BRIDGING THE GAP
A Future Security Architecture
for the Middle East

BRIDGING THE GAP
A Future Security Architecture
for the Middle East

Shai Feldman and Abdullah Toukan

CARNEGIE COMMISSION ON PREVENTING DEADLY CONFLICT

CARNEGIE CORPORATION OF NEW YORK

ROWMAN & LITTLEFIELD PUBLISHERS, INC.
Lanham • Boulder • New York • Oxford

ROWMAN & LITTLEFIELD PUBLISHERS, INC.

Published in the United States of America
by Rowman & Littlefield Publishers, Inc.
4720 Boston Way, Lanham, Maryland 20706

12 Hid's Copse Road
Cummor Hill, Oxford OX2 9JJ, England

British Cataloging in Publication Information Available

Library of Congress Cataloging-in-Publication Data
Feldman, Shai, 1950—
    Bridging the gap : a future security architecture for the Middle
East / Shai Feldman and Abdullah Toukan.
        p.   cm.
    Includes bibliographical references and index.
    ISBN 0-8476-8550-0 (cloth :alk. paper).—ISBN 0-8476-8551-9
(pbk. : alk. paper)
        1. National security—Middle East.   2. Middle East—Defenses.
3. Arms control—Middle East.   I. Toukan, Abdullah. II. Title.
UA832.F45   1997
355'.033056—dc21   97-3920
                                                              CIP

Printed in the United States of America

∞ ™ The paper used in this publication meets the minimum requirements of
American National Standard for Information Sciences—Permanence of Paper for
Printed Library Materials, ANSI Z39.48–1984.

ABOUT THE
Carnegie Commission on Preventing Deadly Conflict Series

Carnegie Corporation of New York established the Carnegie Commission on Preventing Deadly Conflict in May 1994 to address the threats to world peace of intergroup violence and to advance new ideas for the prevention and resolution of deadly conflict. The Commission is examining the principal causes of deadly ethnic, nationalist, and religious conflicts within and between states and the circumstances that foster or deter their outbreak. Taking a long-term, worldwide view of violent conflicts that are likely to emerge, it seeks to determine the functional requirements of an effective system for preventing mass violence and to identify the ways in which such a system could be implemented. The Commission is also looking at the strengths and weaknesses of various international entities in conflict prevention and considering ways in which international organizations might contribute toward developing an effective international system of nonviolent problem solving. The series grew out of the research that the Commission has sponsored to answer the three fundamental questions that have guided its work: What are the problems posed by deadly conflict and why is outside help often necessary to deal with these problems? What approaches, tasks, and strategies appear most promising for preventing deadly conflict? What are the responsibilities and capacities of states, international organizations, and private and nongovernmental organizations for undertaking preventive action?

Published in the series:

BRIDGING THE GAP:
A FUTURE SECURITY ARCHITECTURE FOR THE MIDDLE EAST
by Shai Feldman and Abdullah Toukan

Forthcoming:

The Ambivalence of the Sacred: Religion, Violence, and Reconciliation
   By Scott Appleby
Turkey's Kurdish Question
   By Henri J. Barkey and Graham E. Fuller
The Price of Peace: Incentives and International Conflict Prevention
   Edited by David Cortright
Opportunities Missed, Opportunities Seized: Preventive Diplomacy in the Post-Cold War World
   Edited by Bruce Jentleson
Sustainable Peace: The Role of the UN and Regional Organizations
   By Connie Peck

Reports available from the Commission:

David Hamburg, *Preventing Contemporary Intergroup Violence.* Founding Essay of the Commission. April 1994.

David Hamburg, *Education for Conflict Resolution.* April 1995.

Comprehensive Disclosure of Fissionable Materials: A Suggested Initiative, June 1995.

Larry Diamond, *Promoting Democracy in the 1990s: Actors and Instruments, Issues and Imperatives,* December 1995.

Andrew J. Goodpaster, *When Diplomacy Is Not Enough: Managing Multinational Military Interventions,* July 1996.

Jane E. Holl, *Carnegie Commission on Preventing Deadly Conflict: Second Progress Report,* July 1996.

John Stremlau, *Sharpening International Sanctions: Toward a Stronger Role for the United Nations,* November 1996.

To order *Power Sharing and International Mediation in Ethnic Conflicts* by Timothy Sisk, copublished by the Commission and the United States Institute of Peace, please contact USIP Press, P.O. Box 605, Herndon, VA 22070, USA; (phone) 1-800-868-8064 or 1-703-661-1590.

Full text or summaries of these reports are available on Carnegie Corporation's Web Site: http://www.carnegie.org

To order a report or to be added to the Commission's mailing list, contact:
Carnegie Commission on Preventing Deadly Conflict
2400 N Street, N.W.
Sixth Floor
Washington, D.C. 20037-1153
Phone: (202) 429-7979   Fax: (202) 429-9291
E-mail: pdc@carnegie.org

Members of the Carnegie Commission on Preventing Deadly Conflict

Contents

Acknowledgments   xi

Preface   xiii

Chapter 1

Background for Peace   1
Shai Feldman and Abdullah Toukan

Chapter 2

Israel's National Security: Perceptions and Policy   7
Shai Feldman

Chapter 3

Arab National Security Issues: Perceptions and Policies   33
Abdullah Toukan

Chapter 4

Bridging the Gap: Resolving the Security Dilemma in the
    Middle East   73
Shai Feldman and Abdullah Toukan

Appendix A	97
Appendix B	103
Abbreviations	109
Glossary	111
Index	117
About the Authors	125

Acknowledgments

We would like to express our deep gratitude to Carnegie Corporation and to the Carnegie Commission on Preventing Deadly Conflict for making this enterprise possible. We are especially grateful to David Hamburg, president of Carnegie Corporation, David Speedie, program chair, Preventing Deadly Conflict, Jane Holl, executive director of the Commission, and John Stremlau, advisor to the executive director, for their encouragement and support. We also deeply appreciate the devotion and commitment of Yvonne Schilz and Brian George of the Commission's administrative staff in helping put together the workshop held in Cyprus in August 1995 to discuss the first draft of this document. The devotion and skills of Michael Firillas, currently a Ph.D. student in Middle East history at Harvard University, were a key to the success of the workshop. We would also like to thank Esther Brimmer and Robert Lande of the Commission staff for helping bring our draft to publication. Finally, a special thanks to Sidney Drell of Stanford University. If it were not for his support, this endeavor would have never materialized.

Shai Feldman would like to express special thanks to the Ford Foundation and to the Ploughshares Foundation for supporting his research on the prospects for arms control in the Middle East. Many of the ideas he was able to contribute to this volume were the result of his work from 1989 to 1994 as director of the project on Regional Security and Arms Control in the Middle East at Tel Aviv University's Jaffee Center for Strategic Studies. The financial assistance provided by the two foundations enabled him to conduct this research. In this context, he is especially grateful to the foundation officials who have taken part in providing this assistance: Enid Schoettle, Steven Riskin, Shepard Forman, Geoffrey Wiseman, and Christine Wing at the Ford Foundation, and Sally Lillienthal and Karen Harris at the Ploughshares Foundation.

The last revisions of this manuscript were made after Shai Feldman had begun his term as senior research fellow at Harvard University's Center for Science and International Affairs (CSIA) at the John F. Kennedy School of Government. He would like to express his deep gratitude to Graham Allison and Steven Miller for encouraging and supporting this work.

Abdullah Toukan would like to express particular gratitude to H.R.H. Crown Prince El-Hasan for the encouragement and support he gave to this project. He would also like to thank his wife, Ginny, for her continued support.

Preface

THIS SHORT DOCUMENT is the first attempt by an Israeli scholar and a Jordanian scholar to collaborate in suggesting an architecture for enhancing security in the Middle East. The first chapter, written jointly, describes the background for this document—the Middle East peace process and the Middle East Arms Control and Regional Security (ACRS) talks. It also discusses alternative modes for delineating the Middle East.

In the next two chapters, we provide the building blocks for the proposed architecture. These chapters were written separately and chart Arab and Israeli approaches to security: threat perceptions, the strategies to withstand these threats, and arms control. We also describe Arab and Israeli views with regard to the changes that have taken place in the Middle East security environment in recent years and analyze the effects that these changes might have on strategies and arms control policies.

These building blocks lead to the final chapter in which we suggest how Arabs and Israelis might resolve their security dilemma. Written jointly, it first highlights the remaining gaps between the security concerns of the regions' states as well as between their different approaches to addressing these concerns, and then provides five sets of substantive and structural recommendations for enhancing security in the Middle East.

This document could not have been written without the useful activities conducted since the 1990–91 Gulf War by a number of nongovernmental organizations (NGOs) in convening Arab and Israeli scholars and officials for informal "off-the-record" discussions of the issues related to the region's political and security agenda. Many of these discussions preceded the establishment of formal relations between the countries involved. One such forum, a workshop held by PUGWASH in L'Aquila, Italy, in 1991—some three years before the signing of the Israeli–Jordanian peace treaty—provided the setting for our first meeting. It allowed us an opportunity to exchange views on the Arab--Israeli conflict and to present our perspectives on the possible opportunities for Middle East peace.

Our discovery that we see eye to eye on a number of key security issues of Arab–Israeli peacemaking led to our joint appearance at a May 1992 forum of the Council on Foreign Relations in New York. At a January 1993 meeting held in Delphi, Greece, by the University of California's Institute for Global Conflict and Cooperation (IGCC), we began to discuss the possibility of sketching the common ground between our perspectives on the region's security. We made our final decision to collaborate in September 1994, at the annual meeting of the Washington Institute for Near East Policy, held at the Aspen Institute in Maryland.

Our joint venture was inspired by the short book written by McGeorge Bundy, William Crowe, and Sidney Drell, *Reducing Nuclear Danger*, for the Council on Foreign Relations—a project funded by Carnegie Corporation. We were attracted by the design of their project: collaboration in charting a course for future policy in a concise book.

As a result, we sought the wise council of Sidney Drell, who presented our idea to David Hamburg, president of Carnegie Corporation. Jane Holl, executive director of the Carnegie Commission on Preventing Deadly Conflict, and John Stremlau, advisor to the executive director, also endorsed our suggestion.

In May 1995 the commission asked us to conduct a three-month joint project in the framework of its program. In addition, the commission generously offered to hold a workshop in Cyprus in mid-August 1995, where a number of scholars from Middle East countries reviewed our first draft. We are grateful to these colleagues for contributing their time and energy and for providing useful commentary on our initial thoughts.

It should be emphasized from the outset that we pursued this endeavor solely in our private capacities and as citizens of the Middle East at large. Our respective governments bear no responsibility for our analysis and suggestions. The second and third chapters do not represent "the" Arab and Israeli approaches to the region's security but merely our best understanding of these approaches. Even more important, only we are responsible for the substance and style of our proposals.

A number of additional clarifications are also in order. In the second and third chapters we address Israeli and Arab threat perceptions and security concerns. Intentionally, we refrain from passing any judgment regarding the degree to which these perceptions were justified or not—that is, the extent to which they corresponded with "reality." In our judgment it is too early to attempt such evaluations. Moreover, for our purpose such judgments are largely irrelevant. The point is that these threat perceptions were deeply held by Arabs and Israelis and had important behavioral consequences—first and foremost in defense doctrines and security policies. These behavioral consequences and the extent to which they might be affected by the dramatic changes in the Middle East comprise the central focus of this book.

It should be equally clear that we use very broad strokes when portraying Arab and Israeli threat perceptions, security policies, and approaches to arms control. Largely, we limit ourselves to perceptions and approaches that have been accepted by a majority of Arabs and Israelis. In reality, however, these perceptions and policies are subject to intense internal debates. Indeed, defense policies are often adopted as compromises following considerable bargaining among competing factions that view threats and security differently. Although we were well aware of these debates, we found their details largely irrelevant to the main focus of our work. Security in the Middle East would be greatly enhanced even if only concerns that are widely shared within and among the region's states would be addressed successfully.

The employment of "broad strokes" also applies to changes in Arab and Israeli threat perceptions and security concerns over time. We referred to such changes when they were of extraordinary importance. But since our primary interest is the extent to which the recent expansion of the Arab–Israeli peace process has created new opportunities for enhancing regional security in the Middle East, our abbreviated portraits focus on Arab and Israeli threat perceptions and security policies that, until recently, have remained largely constant.

*   *   *

Since the Gulf War the basic issues troubling the Middle East have not changed. With 5 percent of the world's population, the region's states possess about 60 percent of the world's proven crude oil reserves and account for over 30 percent of the world's arms imports, which makes the Middle

East among the most heavily armed regions. The Middle East also suffers from a chronic shortage of water, one of the world's largest refugee problems, an average annual population growth rate of 3 percent and, as a result, a growing young population seeking employment at a rate much higher than the region's economies can provide. Concern about increasing extremism by both Islamic and Jewish activists, leading at times to terrorism, merely compound these challenges. Since they are regional in character, these problems clearly require regional solutions.

The breakthroughs achieved in bilateral Arab–Israeli negotiations have created for the first time an opportunity to address these problems seriously. Primarily, this refers to the agreements concluded in Oslo, Washington, and Cairo between Israel and the Palestinians in 1993–95, and to the peace treaty signed in October 1994 between Israel and the Hashemite Kingdom of Jordan. Although mostly negotiated outside the formal venues of the 1991 Madrid conference, the agreements were based on the terms of reference of Madrid, primarily United Nations Security Council Resolutions 242 and 338 and the principle of exchanging land for peace.

The assassination of Israeli prime minister Yitzhak Rabin in November 1995 did not stop this process. The agreement signed by Prime Minister Benjamin Netanyahu and Palestinian Authority President Yasir Arafat in January 1997 charted the course for the further implementation of the Oslo agreements.

We hope that these developments will soon result in further breakthroughs—Israeli–Syrian and Israeli–Lebanese accords, as well as successful "final status" negotiations between Israel and the Palestinians. Such agreements will complete the peace process between Israel, the PLO, and all Arab countries adjacent to Israel.

In anticipation of these further breakthroughs, we became convinced that it is time to begin thinking differently about the future of the Middle East. The habits and axioms of a region embedded in hostility should be replaced by a serious examination of the new possibilities for cooperative action aimed at resolving the problems breeding the growing despair in the region.

Attending many meetings between Arabs and Israelis—mostly held by American and European NGOs within the past four years—we became equally persuaded that it would also be tragic if the efforts to address the region's problems were derailed by the desire to end all Middle East miseries simultaneously. This admirable intention resulted in overloading the agenda of some of these meetings and damaging their potential to produce concrete results.

Consequently, while remaining ambitious, we decided to focus on one dimension of the region's affairs: the future of security in the Middle East. We felt that a region enjoying greater security could address its other pressing problems in a more congenial atmosphere. For example, more regional and international private sector investments—and resulting economic development—could be expected in the Middle East as personal security and strategic stability increase.

At the same time, in addressing the region's security agenda, we refrained from second-guessing the negotiations conducted in the framework of the Arms Control and Regional Security (ACRS) working group of the multilateral Arab–Israeli peace negotiations. Similarly, we avoided discussing the many technical details involved in the various issues. Instead, we provide a broad outline of the region's past and future security agenda as well as of the actions required and the most promising avenues to enhance security in the Middle East.

We are fully aware that not all our suggestions could be implemented immediately—some require further positive developments in bilateral Arab–Israeli peacemaking. As noted earlier and elaborated at the end of chapter 4, important gaps between the region's states still need to be bridged. Israeli worry about the extent to which the Arab world is truly prepared to accept a Jewish state as an integral part of the Middle East is matched by Arab concerns regarding the outcome of the prospective "final status" negotiations between Israel and the Palestinians, based on the "land for peace" formula, and Israel's nuclear policy. But the distance that the region has already traveled on the road from war to peace provides conclusive evidence that the time to think differently about the region's security has come and that the problems entailed in bridging the remaining gaps are not insurmountable.

1

Background for Peace

Shai Feldman and Abdullah Toukan

THIS CHAPTER PORTRAYS the background for this document—the developments setting the stage for an examination of the issues and opportunities discussed in this book. It ascertains the present state of the Middle East peace process and elaborates the evolution of the Middle East Arms Control and Regional Security (ACRS) talks. Finally, we define what we mean by "the Middle East" and discuss alternative modes for delineating the region.

Milestones

This book follows seventeen years of peace between Egypt and Israel. The treaty concluded between the two countries in 1979 stipulated that Israel withdraw its armed forces and civilians from the Sinai. The agreement also set the international boundary between Egypt and mandated Palestine as the permanent border between Egypt and Israel. Thus, for the first time the international boundary between an Arab state and Israel was defined. In addition, the treaty established a complex of security arrangements between the two countries—primarily the demilitarization of the Sinai—that were designed to diminish their fear of surprise attack. Despite potentially destabilizing developments such as the assassination of Egypt's president Anwar Sadat and Israel's 1982 invasion of Lebanon, the Egyptian-Israeli treaty stood the test of time remarkably well.

DEFINING THE REGION

What do we mean by the Middle East? What should be the delineation of the region for arms control? A universally accepted definition of the Middle East does not exist. Increasingly, states' approach to defining the region is affected by their threat perceptions. Thus, they are inclined to include all sources of threat within their definition of the region. This tendency has been accelerated by the proliferation of mass destruction weapons and their delivery systems.

Some propose dividing the Middle East into four subregions: the central subregion of states directly involved in the Arab-Israeli conflict, the Gulf subregion that includes all members of the Gulf Cooperation Council (GCC), the Maghreb—the Arab states of North Africa—and the states at the southern tip of the Arabian Peninsula. The main problem with this approach is that states of the Middle East have participated in armed conflict in more than one subregion, as the 1991 Gulf War illustrates.

The U.S. Arms Control and Disarmament Agency (ACDA) defines the region as comprising Bahrain, Cyprus, Egypt, Iran, Iraq, Israel, Jordan, Kuwait, Lebanon, Oman, Qatar, Saudi Arabia, Syria, United Arab Emirates, and Yemen. The CIA's geographical atlas includes Turkey. Both ACDA and the CIA consider Algeria, Libya, Morocco, and Tunisia as part of the African continent. Yet the U.S. Department of State's Near East bureau includes these four states but excludes Cyprus and Turkey. In this context, it is noteworthy that the Arab League includes all the states in the Near East bureau's area of responsibility with the exception of Iran and Israel but including Djibouti, Mauritania, Palestine, Somalia, and Sudan.

Faced with these competing definitions, for our discussion of arms control and regional security, we decided to adopt a delineation of the Middle East that extends from Morocco in the west to Iran in the east, and from Syria in the north to Yemen in the south. This does not preclude the possibility that specific arms control agreements might incorporate only a subset of these countries. Nor does it exclude the possibility that other arms control agreements would require the participation of other states. Thus, the substance and character of the agreement will affect the list of participants.

The post–Gulf War phase of the Middle East peace process was launched at the October 1991 international conference in Madrid, cosponsored by Russia and the United States. Subsequent negotiations were both bilateral and multilateral. Initially, the bilateral Arab-Israeli negotiations were between Israel and Syria, Israel and Lebanon, and Israel and a Jordanian-Palestinian delegation. Soon thereafter, Israeli-Palestinian and Israeli-Jordanian negotiations were separated. By contrast, it became increasingly clear that the fate of Israeli-Lebanese negotiations were tied to the outcome of the Israeli-Syrian talks. Technically, the negotiations are based on United Nations Security Council (UNSC) Resolutions 242 and 338. The Israeli-Lebanese talks are based on UNSC Resolutions 425 and 426. As stipulated in the letters of invitation to the Madrid conference, the goal of the negotiations is comprehensive, just, and lasting peace in the Middle East.

In September 1993 Israel and the Palestine Liberation Organization (PLO) signed a Declaration of Principles (DOP) in Oslo and Washington. Agreements elaborating the first phases of implementing the DOP were subsequently signed in Cairo in May 1994 and in Washington in September 1995. While the first of these inaugurated the Palestinian Authority in Gaza and Jericho, the second established Palestinian self-rule in the West Bank. The latter entails the redeployment of Israeli troops from Palestinian populated areas, the implementation of security arrangements in the West Bank, elections for a Palestinian council, and the transfer of civilian authority (over taxes, water, health care, education, and police, for example) to the Palestinian Authority. By mid-1996 these milestones were followed by the official opening of Israeli-Palestinian final status negotiations on the nature of the Palestinian political entity, its borders with Israel, the future of Jewish settlements in the West Bank and Gaza, the fate of Palestinian refugees, the status of Jerusalem, and final security arrangements.

The murder of Israeli prime minister Yitzhak Rabin by a Jewish assassin in November 1995 and the suicide bombings conducted by Hamas and Islamic Jihad terrorist groups in Tel Aviv and Jerusalem in February–March 1996 did not stop the bilateral process. On January 15, 1997, Prime Minister Benjamin Netanyahu and Palestinian Authority President Yasir Arafat signed an agreement stipulating the further implementation of the Oslo agreements.

In October 1994 Jordan became the second Arab state to sign a peace treaty with Israel. The agreement stipulated the return of Jordanian territory, the delineation and demarcation of the boundaries between the two countries, and a redistribution of the use of water resources.

The multilateral Middle East peace negotiations were launched in January 1992. The first organizational meeting in Moscow formed five working groups on water (chaired by the United States), on the environment (chaired by Japan), on economic development (chaired by the European Community), on refugees (chaired by Canada), and on arms control and regional security (chaired by Russia and the United States). Each working group consists of regional and extraregional parties.

In addition, a multilateral steering committee was formed to overview the peace process. Chaired by Russia and the United States, the committee was designed to monitor progress, to recommend future work such as the issuing of papers defining "a vision" for the region, and to consider the formation of additional working groups, such as a forum for addressing the "human dimension" of the Middle East.

The multilateral working groups have made substantial progress in formulating principles and developing project designs. For example, the Regional Economic Development Working Group (REDWG) completed studies for regional financial mechanisms, tourism associations, and business councils. A major outcome of REDWG was the convening of three Middle East and North Africa economic summit meetings in Morocco in October 1994, in Jordan in October 1995, and in Egypt in October 1996. The environmental working group established codes of conduct and an Upper Gulf of Aqaba oil spill contingency plan. The water working group developed a water data bank system and called for the establishment of a regional desalination research center. The working group on refugees examined issues such as health, child welfare, job creation, human resource development, and family reunification.

The ACRS Process

The ACRS working group was intended to complement the bilateral negotiations and to help create a political environment that would reduce suspicions and promote dialogue between the parties (see appendix A). Israel, the Palestinians, and thirteen Arab states are represented in these talks.

In the framework of the ACRS discussions, arms control combines structural as well as operational dimensions. Structural arms control reduces manpower as well as conventional and unconventional (nuclear, chemical, and biological) weapons, ultimately producing major force-reduction agreements. Operational arms control refers to efforts to prevent war by misunderstanding or miscalculation, to reduce the possibility of surprise attack, and, ultimately, to diminish the ability to use force for the purpose of political intimidation and the execution of foreign policy. Discussions in this realm focus on confidence- and security-building measures (CSBMs) to increase transparency and predictability.

At the conclusion of the ACRS plenary meeting in Moscow in 1993, the parties agreed to divide the process into an "operational basket" to address technical-military CSBMs and a "conceptual basket" to address political-military CSBMs. Technical-military CSBMs are tactical and operational military measures. By contrast, political-military CSBMs are "statements of intent" concerning the use of military forces. Together, CSBMs are designed to influence operational military planning and national security policy.

The operational basket includes maritime CSBMs, prenotification of military activities, exchange of military information, and the establishment of a regional communication network. The conceptual basket includes an effort to define long-term objectives on arms control and regional security, the establishment of a regional security center, verification and monitoring of arms control agreements, and other issues related to civil defense, public awareness, and military contacts and visits. It also includes seminars on topics such as the delineation of the Middle East region for the purposes of arms control, regional security arrangements, prerequisites for initiating structural arms control negotiations, military doctrines and concepts of deterrence, and threat perceptions and security concerns. It was also agreed that multilateral CSBMs as well as all other arms control measures would be implemented on a voluntary and reciprocal basis.

To increase maritime security, the ACRS working group has drafted a regional agreement on the avoidance of incidents at sea as well as on the requirements for search-and-rescue operations. A draft regional agreement on prenotification of military activities and exchange of information was negotiated, similar to the format adopted by the Organization for Security and Cooperation in Europe (OSCE). A communication system for the Middle East based in Egypt—similar to the OSCE communication hub in The Hague—is being studied.

The parties to the ACRS talks also decided to establish a Regional Security Center (RSC) in Jordan, with related facilities in Qatar and Tunis. Initially, the RSC is designed to host and facilitate seminars that support the ACRS process and provide training and education on arms control. It is intended to function as an integral part of the ACRS communication and data bank systems and ensure their compatibility.

The parties' efforts to conclude a Statement on Arms Control and Regional Security have become an important milestone in the ACRS process. The draft statement provided a political basis for formulating a new regionwide code of conduct and elaborated a working agenda on region-specific operational and structural arms control measures. The draft text comprises fundamental principles governing the future security relations among the region's states, guidelines for the ACRS process, and statements of intent regarding the objectives of the ACRS process.

Efforts to adopt the statement failed because of the remaining gaps between the Egyptian and Israeli approaches to controlling weapons of mass destruction. Arab and Israeli participants in the ACRS process agreed that the statement should call for the establishment of a zone free of weapons of mass destruction, including nuclear, chemical, and biological weapons as well as their delivery systems. The Egyptian delegation argued, however, that as a first step toward achieving this objective, all the region's states should adhere to the 1968 nuclear Non-Proliferation Treaty (NPT). By contrast, Israel rejected the possibility that the statement would contain a direct obligation to adhere to the treaty (see appendix B for alternative language proposed by the two parties as well as by the United States). At the closing of the 1994 ACRS plenary meeting in Tunis, this disagreement was the only remaining obstacle to the adoption of the statement.

2

Israel's National Security: Perceptions and Policy

Shai Feldman

THIS CHAPTER DESCRIBES the evolution of Israel's approach to its security problems and outlines its future strategy. The chapter begins with an analysis of the Israelis' view of the threats posed by their Arab neighbors as well as by other players in the Middle East and describes the grand strategy that Israel adopted to cope with its hostile environment. The next section is an analysis of Israel's perceptions of the changes experienced in the Middle East over the past two decades and their likely development in the future. Finally, the chapter describes the effects of these changes on Israel's future security policy and its approach to arms control.

Israel's Perceptions of Its Security Environment

Three premises have guided the Israelis' approach to their nation's security. First, their Arab neighbors were hostile to Zionism, the return of Jews to the Land of Israel. While the founders of Zionism failed to anticipate this opposition, early Israeli leaders and their followers came to view this hostility as very deep and nearly immutable. Thus, while Israel's first prime minister, David Ben Gurion, believed that "an alliance with the Arabs" might be possible at some future point, he regarded Arab hostility as extremely intense in the short and intermediate term.

Israel viewed the extent and possible ramifications of Arab hostility differently from relations between most other countries. In most cases, hostility is limited by the finite character of the issues, such as the location of boundaries or the distribution of resources. These disputes can be resolved, even if violently, without threatening the existence of any of the states involved. By contrast, Israelis regarded the Arab states as hostile to the very existence of their state and as determined to make every attempt to destroy it.

Moreover, the murdering of six million Jews by Nazi Germany during the Second World War reinforced Israeli fears that due to the Arabs' deep hostility, the defeat of the Israeli Defense Forces (IDF) might well lead to total annihilation. Indeed, the only serious debate in Israel regarding this matter focused on whether there was a limit to the price that Arab states would be willing to pay to destroy Israel.

The second premise informing Israeli strategy was that the Middle East and the international system are both anarchic: no single agent enjoys a monopoly of force that would ensure the survival, security, and peace of the various states. Hence, Israel could not rely on any international organization or country to guarantee its existence in the face of Arab hostility. The reluctance of the world powers to help Jews before and during the Second World War reinforced this view. Thus, even the United States is perceived as having refused to allow massive Jewish immigration in the 1930s and as having refrained from bombing Nazi concentration camps in the early 1940s. This history left a permanent imprint on Israeli strategic thinking.

The Israelis' awareness of the anarchic international system increased as they observed the failure of the United Nations to guarantee Israel's survival. The UN General Assembly voted in November 1947 to create a Jewish state by partitioning Palestine, but when Israel was declared in May 1948 and five Arab states invaded, the UN did not defend Israel. By the mid-1990s the failure to stop "ethnic cleansing" in Bosnia provided Israelis with another reminder of the international community's anarchic character.

The third basic perception affecting almost every facet of Israeli efforts to cope with Arab hostility was that in all categories of national power, the Arab countries enjoyed a quantitative advantage—a situation that Ben Gurion described as "the few against the many." This asymmetry manifested itself in the size of populations and armed forces, in territory and strategic depth, in natural resources—primarily oil—and the resulting financial capacity to pay for advanced arms, and in the number of states and the ability to influence international organizations.

The most important imbalance resulting from these many asymmetries was that a successful Arab military campaign could "drive Israelis to the sea"—as Egypt's president Gamal Abdel Nasser threatened to do on the eve of the 1967 war. By contrast, Israel lacked the ability to decide the Arab–Israeli conflict militarily. It could win successive campaigns, but the Arab states were too many and their territory and population were too large for Israel to force their surrender.

Consequently, Israelis became hypersensitive to any development that might encourage their Arab neighbors to attempt a decisive strike. Within this general framework, Israelis manifested a number of particular concerns regarding the implications of their strategic environment. First, largely due to the absence of strategic or even tactical depth, Israel became extremely sensitive to the danger of surprise attack. To compensate for the asymmetry in population size, Israelis were compelled to adopt a military reserve system. Hence, they were deeply concerned that without ample warning, large Arab forces would be able to strike the IDF's small standing force decisively and would be able to continue their assault or fortify their initial gains before the bulk of the IDF's force structure could be mobilized.

This fear was underscored by the strategic surprise Israel experienced at the opening stages of the 1973 war. Many Israelis speculated that had they suffered such a surprise along Israel's pre-1967 borders (rather than along the Suez Canal and on the Golan Heights), the very existence of their state would have been seriously jeopardized.

The many asymmetries mentioned earlier created an Israeli concern that the risks entailed in absorbing a first strike were too high. The total absence of strategic depth as well as the shortage of tactical depth around the country's central core—where the vast majority of Israel's population and most of its industrial infrastructure are located—created fear that Israel might not be able to recover following an assault. For this reason Israelis particularly feared an attack from the east, despite the fact that their country faced much more formidable adversaries in the southwest (Egypt) and the north (Syria). Israel's "soft belly" and its long and winding pre-1967 border with Jordan made it especially sensitive to its "eastern front" problem. This sensitivity was exacerbated by the perceived danger that Israel's close neighbors would attempt to further widen the quantitative gap by gaining external support. Israeli leaders and defense analysts were particularly troubled by the prospect that Iraq might send expeditionary forces to support Jordan's army or to fight alongside the Syrian armed forces. A widely held assessment was that Iraq could contribute seven or eight armored or mechanized divisions to such an effort without excessively weakening its forces on the Iranian front.

Another Israeli security concern focused on the extent to which the larger Arab populations—which could absorb more casualties than Israel—would entice the Arab states to attempt to drag Israel into prolonged warfare. Given its sensitivity to costs, Israel regarded a war of attrition—similar to the warfare initiated by Egypt along the Suez Canal in 1968—with enormous anxiety.

Yet another perceived vulnerability involved the chronic shortage of water. Israel depends in large measure on water sources that are mainly located beyond the pre-1967 frontiers: the aquifer located partly under the West Bank and the water sources of the north located in the Golan Heights and beyond. In 1964–65 this issue became the focus of a violent confrontation between Israel and Syria—contributing to the escalation that later led to the June 1967 war.

Securing adequate supplies was another source of Israeli worries. Indeed, Israel's small population and industrial infrastructure made it especially sensitive to interference with its supply routes and concerned that the country's ability to obtain essential goods in time of war might be jeopardized. Furthermore, the Arab states' superior diplomatic clout—resulting from their larger numbers and their ability to affect the supply and price of oil—induced considerable anxiety that during war these states might persuade external suppliers to deny Israel essential products.

In the longer range, Israelis feared that the Arab states might supplement their numerical advantage by improving the quality of their forces. During the past three decades, this concern assumed varying forms. At first, attention was given to the vast number of graduates from universities in the Arab states. During the 1973 war, for example, Israelis observed that following Egypt's post-1967 decision to place thousands of university graduates in combat units, there was a dramatic improvement in its armed forces. Another Israeli lesson from the 1973 war was that, if well rehearsed, Arab officers and soldiers fought effective set battles despite being less skillful than their Israeli counterparts.

A related Israeli worry was that modern weapons systems—particularly precision-guided munitions—would reduce the importance of the human factor in battle. Arab states bought these weapons in large numbers with revenue from oil sales. This was seen as allowing Arab armed forces the potential to overcome the qualitative edge of the Israeli Defense Forces' soldiers and junior officers.

Another concern was that Arab states might attempt to close the qualitative gap by obtaining or developing weapons of mass destruction (WMD) and the means for these weapons' delivery. This fear first emerged in the mid-1960s when Egypt attempted to recruit German scientists and engineers to develop rockets and nuclear weapons, and when Egypt used chemical weapons during the war in Yemen. In the late 1970s this worry was revived by Iraq's ambitious nuclear program. After the 1991 Gulf War, Israelis were shocked to discover how close Saddam Hussein had come to possessing a nuclear device.

Many Israelis are terrified by the possibility that an Arab state or Iran might possess nuclear weapons. Israelis fear that nuclear weapons may rekindle the Arab dream of ending the Arab–Israeli conflict by force, through a nuclear "first strike" aimed at Israel's total destruction. Indeed, Israelis fear that the prospects of eliminating their country may prove too enticing for Arab leaders to ignore, even in the face of possible Israeli retaliation.

Closely related to this fear is the conviction of many Israelis that Arab leaders may behave irrationally and that, therefore, it would be difficult to deter them from using their nuclear weapons. Another concern involves the possibility that Arab states may not possess adequate means to control the weapons at their disposal, thus raising the danger of accidental use. Israel is extremely vulnerable to nuclear attack because its small population is concentrated in a few urban areas. Thus, it is hardly surprising that Israelis regard the possible possession of nuclear weapons by an Arab state or Iran as a potential catastrophe.

Israel's perceived vulnerability, coupled with the experience of the Holocaust—when millions of Jews were gassed to death—created a unique Israeli fear of chemical and biological attacks. This collective memory induces Israelis to fear such attacks, particularly if executed with ballistic missile warheads, almost as much as nuclear attacks.

Of course, Israelis are particularly concerned about relations with their Palestinian neighbors. For some Israelis the Palestinians presented an on-going challenge to their ability to reclaim their historical rights over the entire Land of Israel. For the majority of Israelis, however, who were more pragmatic, an independent Palestinian state near Israel's "soft belly" raised four concerns. First, Israelis feared that a Palestinian state located so close to Israel's center would become a springboard for an Arab assault. Thus, the West Bank was seen as a potential staging area for the armies of other Arab states. Second, it was feared that a Palestinian state would manifest irredentist designs—seeking to regain control over land lost in the 1948 war. A clear manifestation of such possible designs involves the Palestinians' commitment to "the right of return" of Palestinian refugees to reestablish communities left before and during the war. A third major source of concern entails the possible "Lebanonization" of the Palestinian state—the collapse of central authority under the weight of internal struggles. Various factions would continue their opposition to the Jewish state through terrorism, and there would be no single authority against which Israel could practice deterrence. Finally, there was deep concern that the creation of an independent Palestinian state would encourage Israel's significant Arab minority to demand "cultural autonomy" within the Jewish state. It was further feared that this would eventually lead Israeli Arabs to demand political autonomy—which would threaten Israel's integrity as a sovereign state.

Israel's Grand Strategy

To cope with its hostile environment and to address its security concerns in the absence of external guarantors, Israel adopted a grand strategy based on the principle of self-help. Primarily, this strategy was designed to overcome the various facets of the Arabs' quantitative advantages.

Unable to resolve the Arab–Israeli conflict in its favor by military means, Israel pursued a strategy of cumulative deterrence, hoping that a long record of failure to defeat Israel militarily would persuade Arab leaders that there was no alternative to political accommodation. In the absence of expectations that any specific military action might induce the Arab states to accept Israel as a permanent feature of the Middle East, Israel adopted a strategy to obtain this goal incrementally.

To offset the Arabs' perceived greater numbers, Israel sought to develop a qualitative edge in all civilian and military realms: the education provided to its citizens, the expertise of its scientists and engineers, the level of military and civilian research and development, the quality of the weapons systems purchased and produced, military tactics and the art of war, and the personal initiative and strong motivation among the IDF's soldiers as well as junior and midlevel officers.

The challenge of facing "the many" created an absolute imperative that "the few" would remain united. This would ensure the high morale and strong motivation of Israel's soldiers and officers. The resulting principle of Israel's grand strategy—maintaining its "unity of purpose"—broke down soon after the 1967 war, when Israelis became embroiled in a debate over the occupation of the conquered territories. The focus of the debate was the justification and wisdom of attempting to control almost two million Palestinians who rejected Israeli occupation, at first passively and later violently.

A major facet of the imperative that unity of purpose would be maintained was the requirement that war would be waged only if there were "no choice." Israeli prime minister Menachem Begin violated this principle when he explicitly invoked the right to wage war "by choice" during Israel's invasion of Lebanon in 1982. The disastrous domestic consequences of this invasion underscored the importance of maintaining the nation's cohesion.

In the military, adhering to the principle that war would be waged only when there was no choice served to ensure that the determination and morale of the IDF's soldiers and officers would be superior to that of their more numerous enemies. When situations permitted adherence to this principle—the May–June 1967 crisis and war provide the best example— the results of the confrontation were decisively favorable. Conversely, when Israel was challenged by more-determined adversaries, the outcome was unfavorable. This was illustrated persuasively when the Lebanese Shiites resisted Israeli control over large parts of southern Lebanon in 1983–84 and when the Palestinians launched the Intifada against Israel in the West Bank and Gaza in December 1987.

The high motivation of Israel's citizens and soldiers at the height of the Arab–Israeli conflict was inspired by a factor mentioned earlier—their perception that because Arab hostility was so deep, defeat might well result in their nation's annihilation. Reinforced by the experience of the Second World War, Israeli soldiers thought that they were fighting to prevent a second Holocaust in May–June 1967. While this was not the only factor determining the outcome of the war, its contribution to Israel's victory was considerable.

Parallel to ensuring that "the few" remain united, Israel also encouraged disunity among "the many." Thus, Israel dealt with its more numerous neighbors by separating them as much as possible in wartime as well as in peace negotiations. In war this implied making every attempt to defeat the Arab states sequentially to avoid confronting several simultaneously. Thus, during the 1948, 1967, and 1973 wars, the IDF shifted its main effort from front to front, trying to compel Israel's adversaries to seek a cease-fire one by one.

Similarly, in advancing the prospects of peace, Israel attempted to avoid international conferences in which it might have faced a united Arab front that would be influenced by the most hard-line of the Arab states. Hence, it made every attempt to negotiate peace agreements bilaterally, separately, and sequentially, and it rejected the imposition of linkages that might have made the process hostage to the preferences of the least cooperative party.

Another facet of Israel's grand strategy was external alliances to overcome its numerical disadvantage. Such alliances were not regarded as a substitute for self-reliance but rather as a supplement to the self-help measures that Israel adopted. Within this framework, it made efforts to create three types of alliances: with a great power, primarily the United States, with states on the periphery of the Middle East, and with minorities in the region.

When Ben Gurion's efforts to conclude an alliance with Washington in the early 1950s failed, he turned to France in 1955. This resulted in a decade of intense French–Israeli defense cooperation leading to the advanced Israeli military machine that triumphed in 1956 and 1967, as well as the development of Israel's nuclear option.

When President Charles de Gaulle ended the French–Israeli alliance in 1967, Israel turned again to the United States. Beginning in 1970 and especially after 1983, Israeli–U.S. relations developed into a partnership including combined strategic planning, joint military exercises, the prepositioning of U.S. weapons and ammunition in Israel, U.S. acquisition of military equipment from Israel, and Israeli participation in state-of-the-art U.S. research and development projects, notably the Strategic Defense Initiative (SDI, later renamed the Ballistic Missile Defense Organization, BMDO), as well as cooperation in the development of less-powerful weapons.

Earlier, during the 1950s and 1960s, Israel created close ties with states on the periphery of the Arab–Israeli conflict area: Turkey in the north, Ethiopia in the south, and Iran in the east. An important objective of these efforts was to prevent Arab states from devoting all their resources to confronting Israel. These alliances also demonstrated to hostile neighbors the gains that they might derive from cooperating with Israel.

Alliances with minorities had a similar objective. The small Jewish community in the Middle East attempted to support other minorities in the region: the Maronite Christians in Lebanon, the Christians in south Sudan, and the Kurds in Iraq. The purpose of this was to ensure that the troubles brewed by these minorities would cause the governments of the Arab states to direct their energies away from the conflict with Israel.

Israel's small population and the intimacy characteristic of its social and family networks resulted in an extreme sensitivity to casualties. Thus, Israel made every effort to avoid war through deterrence pursued at a number of levels simultaneously. With conventional weapons, Israel attempted to deter war by warning Arab states that the IDF would quickly repulse their attack, pursue their forces, and destroy them on their own territory. This was crystallized in the phrase coined by then IDF chief of staff, Lt. Gen. Yitzhak Rabin: "The purpose of the IDF is to deter war, and if deterrence fails, to decide the battle and to destroy the attacking forces in the adversary's territory." Thus, the prospects of defeat and the costs involved in the destruction of their armed forces were expected to dissuade Arab leaders from launching conventional wars against the Jewish state.

A particular facet of Israel's conventional deterrence involved its efforts to dissuade the introduction of expeditionary forces into staging areas from which an attack on the Jewish state might be launched. Israel's efforts in this realm involved primarily its declared policy stipulating that the introduction of Iraqi forces into Jordan would lead to war. They also involved understandings and tacit agreements with Israel's neighbors, sometimes worked out through third parties. The clearest example of these agreements was the tacit Israeli–Syrian "red lines" understanding mediated in 1976 by U.S. secretary of state Henry Kissinger. The agreement stipulated a line in southern Lebanon beyond which Syria would not introduce its forces. (The agreement contained additional limitations, such as Syria's consent to refrain from using its air force in Lebanon.) Israel reinforced the understanding by sending deterrent messages when Syria attempted on a number of occasions to probe Israel's commitment by moving small forces south of the line.

Israel attempted to deter terrorist attacks by maintaining "escalation dominance"—that is, the ability to cause far greater damage to the terrorists and their sponsors than the damage that the terrorists could cause. Retaliatory, preventive, and preemptive strikes were designed to deter and compel: to deter terrorist attacks directly and to compel host countries to stop terrorism launched from their territory. In retrospect, this strategy seems to have worked best when such hosts had a strong interest in avoiding the consequences of Israeli escalation dominance (Jordan in 1954 and Syria in Lebanon throughout most of the past two decades). It failed completely when these hosts were interested in such escalation (Egypt in 1953–55, largely due to President Nasser's inter-Arab considerations) or were too weak to stop terrorism (the Lebanese government after 1970).

Israel often had to make difficult choices in implementing its deterrence strategy. For example, Syrian forces in Lebanon might have been better able to stop terrorist incursions against Israel had they been permitted to move closer to the Israeli–Lebanese border. Yet such proximity could have provided these forces better staging areas from which they could attack Israel in case of war. Hence, Israel insisted that Syria comply with the 1976 tacit "red lines" agreement.

Israel's ambiguous nuclear posture was another facet of its deterrence strategy. This ambiguity was based on the development of a nuclear potential coupled with the public commitment to refrain from being "the first country to introduce nuclear weapons into the Middle East." Some Israeli leaders added that their state would "not become the second, either"—implying that Israel would not be far behind any state that did introduce such weapons into the region. This left ambiguous what Israelis meant by the terms "introduce," and "the Middle East." Referring to this ambiguity and its role in Israeli strategy, then foreign minister Shimon Peres stated that "nuclear 'fog' was always part of Israel's national security concept."

While conventional escalation dominance was designed to deter low-level challenges to Israel's security, the ambiguous nuclear posture was intended to deter threats to Israel's existence. It ensured that the Arab states could not rule out the possibility that an assault aimed at destroying the Jewish state would result in unacceptable retaliation.

In maintaining their ambiguous nuclear posture, Israeli leaders seem to have been motivated by a number of considerations. First, they wanted to avoid encouraging the Arab states to acquire a nuclear capability. The Israelis probably feared that the adoption of explicit deterrence would produce enormous domestic pressures on Arab leaders to acquire nuclear weapons and legitimize nuclear transfers to Arab countries by Chinese, European, and Russian suppliers.

Possibly more important, Israel's nuclear ambiguity prevented a head-on collision with U.S. nuclear nonproliferation policy and legislation by providing the United States with a measure of "plausible deniability." Thus, ambiguity allowed U.S. administrations to avoid applying to Israel legislation stipulating a ban on economic and military assistance to countries that acquired a nuclear capability.

More generally, Israel had no desire to challenge the international norms against the spread of nuclear weapons. In contrast to India, which also maintains nuclear ambiguity, Israel did not dispute the rationale of the nuclear Non-Proliferation Treaty (NPT). It only viewed the application of the treaty as flawed and reasoned that signing the treaty would not be in its best interests. Primarily, Israel could not sign the NPT because the application of the treaty's safeguards would have required it to abandon its ambiguous posture.

At the conventional military level, Israel made every attempt to overcome its smaller population base while avoiding a paralysis of its civilian economy by developing an efficient reserve and call-up system. Thus, a large part of Israel's potential "order of battle" was held in reserve during peacetime. The fact that only a fraction of Israel's forces were normally mobilized while Arab forces were almost entirely fully mobilized—thus exposing Israel to the threat of surprise attack—induced enormous investments in Israel's intelligence community to reduce the odds of such a surprise.

In the event that deterrence failed and war needed to be waged, Israel's defense required the adoption of a highly offensive military doctrine. Israel's vulnerability—its small size, the density of its small population, the lack of tactical depth, and the total absence of operational and strategic depth—created an absolute imperative to transfer hostilities to the adversary's territory as quickly as possible. Thus, the IDF's almost reflexive emphasis on the offense was propelled primarily by a sense of exposure and vulnerability—not by inherently aggressive and expansionist designs.

Indeed, this sense of vulnerability propelled Israel to take preventive measures well before threats materialized. For example, Israel participated in the Anglo–French 1956 assault on Egypt before the large quantity of arms purchased by Egypt from Czechoslovakia in late 1955 could be put into operation. Some twenty-five years later the same rationale induced Israel to destroy Iraq's Osiraq nuclear research reactor.

Israel also made preemptive strikes when it perceived that an attack was imminent. For example, Israel bombed Egypt's airfields and sent ground forces to destroy the Egyptian army in the Sinai in early June 1967. Similarly, Israel conducted numerous preemptive raids against terrorist bases throughout the past four decades.

To "deliver the battle to the adversary's territory" and conduct preemptive and preventive strikes, the IDF emphasized high mobility in its military doctrine and force structure. On the ground this translated into the emphasis on armor—tanks and armored personnel carriers—as well as on helicopter-borne combat units. In the air it required enormous investments in Israel's air force, which was equipped with state-of-the-art aircraft and weapons systems.

The centrality of airpower in Israeli strategy resulted from a number of additional considerations. First, addressing Israel's fear of surprise attack required forces that could be mobilized and deployed within minutes to stop the attackers until the ground forces could be mobilized and sent to the front. Second, the possibility that Israel would face an Arab coalition along all its borders required forces that could be rapidly shifted from one front to another. In both of these roles there was no substitute for airpower.

After the 1967 war Israel added another facet to its national security policy: the concept of defensible borders. Coined by Prime Minister Golda Meir, the term implied an effort to improve the pre-1967 borders—then regarded as making Israel too vulnerable and hence too tempting a target. Defensible borders would be farther away from Israel's main population and industrial centers.

Israel's post-1967 government never made clear what it would demand in prospective negotiations with the Arab states to obtain defensible borders. But the "adjustment" involved was widely understood to allow Israel minimal tactical depth in the West Bank, the Golan Heights, and the Sinai.

In summary, Israel adopted a strategy to cope with the various threats that it perceived. The strategy comprised developing a qualitative edge, deterring attack with conventional and unconventional threats, and adopting an offensive military doctrine and force structure. The purpose of Israel's grand strategy was to establish a record of Arab failures to defeat Israel in the hope that the cumulative effect of these failures would persuade Arab leaders that Israel cannot be destroyed, that the Arab–Israeli conflict cannot be decided militarily, and that, consequently, there was no better alternative to resolving the conflict through negotiations.

The New Regional Environment

By the early 1990s the international and regional environment was significantly transformed. This change was partly the result of the success of Israel's grand strategy and partly the consequence of external factors. Three developments seem to have been the milestones leading to the "new Middle East": the end of the Cold War, the Gulf War, and the beginning of peace negotiations. From Israel's standpoint the new Middle East environment is increasingly a struggle between two conflicting forces: the unprecedented progress made in the bilateral and multilateral peace process and developments that threaten to destroy the very foundations of this process.

The Peace Process

The end of the Cold War and the breakup of the Soviet Union terminated—or at least suspended indefinitely—superpower competition in the region. This was first reflected in Moscow's refusal to continue guaranteeing radical Arab regimes such as that of Mu'ammar Gadhafi in Libya. It was also manifested in President Mikhail Gorbachev's suggestion to President Hafez el-Assad of Syria in 1987 that he abandon his quest for strategic parity with Israel and instead resolve the conflict diplomatically. Thus, Arab governments that rejected the Middle East peace process lost their Soviet strategic umbrella and could no longer count on Moscow's intervention in a war with Israel.

Another consequence of the end of the Cold War was the opening of the former Soviet Union's gates to Jewish emigration to Israel, which increased Israel's population by about 15 percent above its normal growth rate in less than four years. In the eyes of a number of Arab observers, Moscow had become the Arabs' de facto adversary, supplying Israel with a critically important resource—more people. This also affected the quantitative and qualitative dimensions of the demographic balance: highly professional immigrants now made Israel more robust than ever.

The 1990–91 Gulf crisis and war had a number of consequences. As the first full-scale invasion of one Arab country by another—leading a coalition of Arab countries to confront the invader—it crystallized Arab disunity and shattered any hope of constructing a unified "eastern front" that could attack Israel. For many Arab observers the Gulf War also reinforced perceptions of a strong Israeli–U.S. alliance. The United States sent Patriot air-defense missile units to Israel—the first time ever that U.S. combat troops helped to defend the Jewish state. Some Arab analysts further reasoned that if the United States confronted Iraq with half a million men in defense of Kuwait, it was likely to make at least as great an effort to defend Israel. (Other Arab observers dispute this view, arguing that the United States was protecting its vital interest in Gulf oil—a consideration that plays no role in the case of threats to Israel's security.)

Finally, the Gulf War demonstrated what a state-of-the-art military force could do to the armed forces of a Middle East regional power. Some Arab observers associate the IDF with the characteristics of such a force structure, which reinforced their assessment that the Israeli army was too strong to be challenged in a full-scale conventional war, and that, consequently, the Arab–Israeli dispute could not be resolved militarily.

The end of the Cold War, the breakup of the Soviet Union, and the Gulf War led to the third milestone: the Madrid bilateral Arab–Israeli peace process and the Moscow multilateral Middle East negotiations. Twelve years after the Egypt–Israel peace agreement, this new stage in regional peacemaking was propelled by Syria's decision to accept the invitation extended to it by U.S. secretary of state James Baker to attend the Madrid conference. The decision reflected Syria's conclusion that in light of Israel's cumulative deterrence (its impressive record of withstanding Arab challenges over four decades), the loss of the Soviet strategic umbrella, and the strength of the Israeli–U.S. alliance, there was no alternative to engaging Israel in direct negotiations.

The loss of the Soviet umbrella and Syria's weaker standing later allowed the Hashemite Kingdom of Jordan to defy Damascus and negotiate a separate peace treaty with Israel. Recognizing that Damascus would not protect Jordan's interests and that Jordan would be in a much weaker position were it to negotiate an agreement with Israel after an Israeli–Syrian agreement was concluded, King Hussein opted for "preemptive peace" with the Jewish state.

Earlier, a major miscalculation by PLO leader Yasir Arafat during the Gulf crisis had paved the way to the Israeli–Palestinian agreements in Oslo, Washington, and Cairo. Viewing Saddam Hussein's invasion of Kuwait as an opportunity to challenge Washington's support of Israel, Arafat sided with Iraq. This was immediately interpreted as an act of betrayal by Saudi Arabia and the smaller Gulf states—the Palestinians' most important political and financial supporters—leading them to suspend assistance to the PLO. Having lost Moscow's support earlier, the PLO now found itself in its weakest position ever, which compelled Arafat to make the painful concession that allowed the Oslo negotiations to succeed: for the first time the PLO accepted an open-ended Israeli–Palestinian peace process, one that was not predicated on an Israeli commitment to Palestinian statehood.

These bilateral breakthroughs were supplemented by multilateral Middle East talks launched by the Moscow conference in early 1992. Israel, the Palestinians, and thirteen Arab governments were represented in these talks addressing regionwide problems: economic development, the environment, water, refugees, and arms control and regional security. If measured by formal agreements reached, not more than modest progress has been made on most of these issues. Yet the manner in which these talks have evolved underscores the dramatic transformation of the Middle East environment.

Threats to the Peace Process

A number of regional developments threaten to destroy the gains made in Arab–Israeli peacemaking. These developments comprise Israel's new threat environment.

The first major threat is that the Middle East peace process could be reversed. One possible cause for such a reversal would be the spread of Islamic extremism supported by Iran (and, to a lesser degree, by the Sudan). While Iran is not seen as likely to possess the conventional force structure to threaten Israel directly, it is supporting terrorist groups that are making every effort to undermine the peace process—Hezbullah in southern Lebanon and Hamas and Islamic Jihad in the West Bank and

Gaza. Forcing Israel to take countermeasures that complicate the implementation of the Israeli–Palestinian accords, such terrorism is viewed as threatening Israel's strategic objectives.

Even more serious, Islamic extremists are increasingly seen as posing a threat to Arab regimes that comprise the core of the Middle East peace process. Fourteen years after Egypt's president Anwar Sadat was assassinated by extremist officers and soldiers, this concern was underscored in June 1995 when Islamic terrorists attempted to assassinate President Hosni Mubarak during a visit to Ethiopia.

At the same time Israelis could observe that Islamist members of the Jordanian parliament rejected the Hashemite Kingdom's peace agreement with Israel. For almost a year they defied their king's initiative to cancel legislation that prohibited economic interaction with the Israelis. In southern Lebanon the military arms of Hezbullah have engaged the IDF and its local allies—the South Lebanese Army—in continuous warfare, extracting a heavy toll from Israel's young soldiers. Meanwhile, the political arm of Hezbullah has transformed itself into a formidable force in the Lebanese parliament. Among the Palestinians, Israel increasingly viewed Hamas as presenting a serious threat to Arafat and as gaining strength based on an impressive capacity to supply social services to an impoverished population. Thus, in Egypt, Jordan, and Lebanon, and among the Palestinians, extremists are seen as posing an increasingly potent challenge to those associated with Arab–Israeli peacemaking.

In this context the possible destabilization of Egypt's government seems particularly terrifying. As the largest, most populous, and most important of the Arab states, only Egypt could pave the way for Middle East peace negotiations in the late 1970s. Israel's fear is that if Egypt's government were toppled by opponents of peace, the course of the peace process in the region might be reversed. Israelis are only partly relieved by Egyptian assurances that support for their government remains robust. The latter view is based on the proposition that the Mubarak government rests on a solid coalition of the military, the rural elite, the government bureaucracy, and the business community.

Israel is also concerned about the consequences of more modest gains by Islamic extremists in Egypt. Indeed, there is considerable concern that an Islamist takeover in Algeria might strengthen the fundamentalists in Egypt and force the Mubarak government to take their priorities much more seriously into account. Such a development would make Egypt far less capable of playing a constructive role in Arab–Israeli peacemaking. Egypt might then be forced to adopt tough positions regarding Israel's conduct, which would threaten gains made in the Middle East peace process.

Israelis' fears about the possible reversibility of the peace process extend beyond their concern about the rising influence of Islamic extremism. The peace process seems to many Israelis to be enjoying thin support among Arab publics. In Israeli eyes, this is reflected in much negative commentary in the Arab press, including semiofficial newspapers such as Egypt's *Al-Ahram* and Jordan's *Al-Ra'y*. It is also manifested in the continued appeal of Nasserist and other Arab nationalist sentiments, which affect the substance and tone of much Arab media reporting on Israel and on issues related to the Arab–Israeli peace process. While Israel does not expect to become immune to Arab press criticism in the "new Middle East," the intensity of Arab media attacks induce Israeli fears that they reflect deeply embedded "old Middle East" thinking. Further evidence of this hostility is the continued boycott of Israel by most Egyptian and Jordanian intellectuals.

More specifically, Israelis fear that a reversal of the peace process might lead Syria to launch another war to compel Israel to withdraw from the Golan Heights at a lesser price than that entailed in the normalization of Syria's relations with Israel and the elaborate security arrangements currently demanded by Israeli negotiators. The operational objectives of such a war would not be to defeat the IDF but rather to cause its retreat from the Golan Heights by extracting high costs from Israel's citizen-soldiers. These high costs would affect the calculations of Israeli leaders with respect to Israel's future control of the Golan.

Related to these concerns is Israel's growing fear of the proliferation of ballistic missiles and weapons of mass destruction to Iran and Iraq. For about fifteen years Saddam Hussein has demonstrated skill and determination in devoting enormous resources to obtaining nuclear weapons. While all known Iraqi nuclear facilities have been destroyed either by coalition bombing during the 1991 Gulf War or by the United Nations Special Commission (UNSCOM) after the war, almost all the scientists and engineers who worked on Iraq's nuclear program (fissile material production and bomb design) remain. Most likely, Saddam Hussein continues to regard his nuclear efforts as a technological and cultural challenge to the

West. Thus, should UNSCOM's monitoring end following the lifting of UN sanctions, Iraq may revive its efforts to obtain nuclear weapons.

Clearly, Iraq may shorten the process were it able to buy fissile material smuggled from the former Soviet Union. Since Iraqi scientists are likely to have continued their clandestine work on a bomb design after the Gulf War, obtaining fissile material is currently Iraq's most difficult barrier to obtaining "the bomb." From 1990 to 1994 there were some indications that significant quantities of fissile material from the former Soviet Union might have been smuggled to the Middle East. The likelihood of this is impossible to determine, but it remains a source of continuous Israeli concern.

In Israeli eyes, fissile material "leaked" to Iran would be even more dangerous. Indeed, by the mid-1990s Israel came to regard Iran as a greater threat than Iraq. While the logic of this assessment was not entirely clear, it seems to be fueled less by evaluation of Iranian behavior and more by Israelis' difficulties in understanding Iran's extremist Islamic regime and its intentions.

Lacking a better alternative, Israelis infer Iran's intentions from the extreme rhetoric of its leaders. Israeli prime minister Shimon Peres has said that Iran perceives Israel "as a collective Salman Rushdie." After Rushdie published *The Satanic Verses* in 1988, Ayatollah Khomeini called for his assassination. Hence, Peres implies that Tehran also seeks Israel's destruction.

In this context Israel interprets the agreement between Iran and Russia to complete the building of two 1300 megawatt nuclear power reactors in Bushehr and to build two additional 440 megawatt reactors as a significant long-term contribution to Iran's efforts to build nuclear weapons. Israel's assessment rests on Iranian statements calling upon Muslims to acquire nuclear weapons and on Iran's interest in buying a uranium enrichment plant from Russia. It is also based on indications that during the past few years, Iran has been attempting to acquire some of the same sensitive materials bought by Iraq in the late 1980s in its efforts to construct uranium enrichment facilities, and on signs that Iran has also attempted to buy fissile material smuggled from the former Soviet Union. A more recent source of concern is that Iran's legitimate purchase of materials required for the completion of its 1300 megawatt reactors at Bushehr would become a smoke screen behind which it would be able to acquire nuclear materials needed for the construction of clandestine fissile material production facilities. Iran's increased interest in a nuclear option is understandable given its post–Gulf War discovery that Iraq was only a few years away from developing nuclear weapons. But two important sets of evidence lead Israelis to fear that the Khomeini regime sees Israel as the target of its nuclear efforts: first, most Iranian statements call for the acquisition of nuclear weapons by Muslim countries because of Israel's nuclear potential. Second, evidence of Iran's financial involvement in North Korea's program to develop and produce the "No-Dong" ballistic missile indicates that Iran insisted that the missile have a range of 1,300 kilometers, which is long enough to reach Israel from Iran.

In addition to nuclear weapons, Israel is concerned about its neighbors' chemical and biological arms and their ability to deliver them with ballistic missiles. This is clearly the case with Syria, which has missiles with sufficient range for reaching every strategic target in Israel.

Most likely, Iraq is also hiding up to two hundred ballistic missiles, possibly equipped with chemical warheads. Although UNSCOM inspectors have attempted to find these stocks and destroy them, Iraq continues to try to deceive the inspectors. For example, in July 1995—after four years of UNSCOM efforts—Baghdad finally admitted that it started a biological weapons program in the 1980s. A few weeks later additional information made available following the defection of Hussein Kamal, a close associate of Saddam Hussein, further exposed Saddam's attempts to hide the full magnitude of Iraq's WMD efforts and the advanced state of its biological weapons program. Similarly, Iran is also suspected of possessing chemical weapons and possibly biological weapons as well. Thus, Iran's possible acquisition of ballistic missiles that could reach Israel is an important concern.

While Israel has withstood the challenges of its previously hostile environment, it now confronts a new set of threats. At the same time, a major change in its standing in the region has clearly taken place. No longer is Israel confronted by a large number of deeply hostile Arab states. Instead, it is now on its way to becoming just another player in the region—even if somewhat more formidable than many of its neighbors. As such, and like the region's other states, Israel can take advantage of the many opportunities of life in the Middle East, but it is also subject to the grave dangers of the region.

Israel's Approach to Arms Control

The transformation of the Middle East security environment caused Israel to define its approach to arms control. Prior to the multilateral negotiations in Moscow in early 1992, Israel did not formulate a comprehensive arms control policy. Instead, it adopted positions with regard to specific items on the global arms control agenda on an *ad hoc* basis.

The discussions and negotiations launched in the framework of the ACRS working group compelled Israel to enter into an intergovernmental consultation process allowing the adoption of a policy with respect to the agenda and content of these talks. This more systematic approach was later also applied to defining Israel's positions with respect to the various facets of the global arms control agenda as they became increasingly salient between 1992 and 1995.

Although Israel has so far refrained from making its arms control policy public in a single comprehensive document, its approach to the various issues can be discerned. This approach is based on a number of principles and preferences: first, that regional arms limitations can be adopted only after reducing tensions and increasing the level of trust among the region's states. Hence, within the framework of the ACRS talks, Israel repeatedly emphasized the importance of applying regional confidence- and security-building measures first.

Israel also insists that *discussions* regarding the possibility of limiting sensitive arms—primarily nuclear arms—should begin only after comprehensive peace has been achieved and minimal levels of confidence and trust have been established. The Israeli government seems to believe that once discussions are initiated, it is difficult to ensure that they do not "slip" into negotiations. In order to avoid the pressures that premature negotiations are likely to produce, Israel prefers to avoid such discussions altogether.

In Israel's eyes it is also unwise to discuss the control of weapons proliferation before all major sources of proliferation are brought into such discussions. In the case of mass destruction weapons, such discussions are futile as long as Iran and Iraq—whose ballistic missile and WMD programs are regarded by Israel as a serious threat—remain outside the ACRS framework.

The Israelis also much prefer regional arms control arrangements to the application of global arms control instruments in the Middle East. Many of these global instruments have proven ineffective, primarily due to the inadequate means of verifying their signatories' compliance. Thus, the 1968 Non-Proliferation Treaty and its associated International Atomic Energy Agency (IAEA) safeguards are regarded as having been repeatedly violated by Iraq, North Korea, and other countries. The Biological Weapons Convention is widely regarded as unverifiable, and there are also serious questions regarding the ability to ensure compliance with the recently adopted Chemical Weapons Convention (CWC).

Israel favors regional arrangements, such as the Tlatelolco Treaty transforming Latin America into a nuclear weapon–free zone (NWFZ). In Israeli thinking, regional arrangements allow the adoption of a more robust verification regime in the framework of which international monitoring can be supplemented by regional multilateral verification mechanisms, by sets of bilateral on-site inspections, and by national technical means (NTMs). Hence, Israeli leaders and senior officials have stated on more than one occasion that once peace is established, discussions should be conducted regarding the possible transformation of the Middle East into a mutually verifiable weapons-of-mass-destruction–free zone (WMDFZ). Wording to this effect was also included in the text of the Israeli–Jordanian peace agreement in October 1994.

Thus, in verifying arms control agreements, Israel demands no less than what the United States and the USSR demanded when they negotiated their bilateral agreements, such as the INF (Intermediate-range Nuclear Forces) treaty and START (Strategic Arms Reduction Treaty): They refused to delegate primary responsibility for the verification of these agreements to an international organization and insisted on mutual verification through on-site inspections and the use of NTMs. This does not preclude international organizations from participating in verifying regional arrangements, but it does mean that their verification should be secondary to the parties' own role in ensuring compliance with the agreements.

Finally, Israel is determined that arms control not be allowed to undermine national security. Thus, as long as Israel faces significant threats, arms control measures that may weaken deterrence must be rejected. Israel's perceived need to maintain its ambiguous nuclear posture led to its continual refusal to sign the NPT and to subject all its nuclear facilities to full-scope IAEA safeguards. Conversely, with regard to chemical weapons—which were not a part of Israeli deterrence—Israel was an original signatory of the CWC. Similarly, in 1994 Israel joined the United Nations General Assembly consensus authorizing the Conference on Disarmament in Geneva to negotiate a treaty banning the production of fissile material for nuclear weapons.

The Future of Israel's Security Policy

Israel's new international and regional environment will require major changes in its grand strategy. While a number of components of the original strategy are likely to remain valid, some new elements may have to be added and different emphasis placed on some of the strategy's original pillars. Most important, Israel would have to make every effort to reduce the likelihood of war by reducing its neighbors' motivation for violence. This will entail continuing to pursue every facet of the Middle East peace process in an attempt to defuse potential sources of conflict. Israel would have to make every effort to complete the ring of peace treaties with its immediate Arab neighbors by concluding peace agreements with Syria and Lebanon.

Aside from diminishing the chances of war with these countries, peace agreements with Syria and Lebanon will have two additional strategic consequences. First, Syria will have an incentive to stop terrorism from Lebanon against Israel because it will not want to get involved in escalation spirals resulting from the activities of Palestinian and Shiite terrorist groups. Since these agreements are likely to signal an overall shift in Syrian policy from its present limited alliance with Iran to improved relations with Europe and the United States, Iran's indirect threat to Israel through its support of Hezbullah in Lebanon is also likely to be curtailed.

At least as important, peace agreements between Israel and its immediate neighbors will significantly erode the political context of any direct threats from Iraq and Iran. While these countries have a growing capacity to strike Israel with ballistic missiles without regard to the position of other states in the region, it is difficult to imagine that they would attack following the transformation of the region's political environment and the resolution of disputes between Israel, Lebanon, and Syria.

Yet reducing tension in the region will also require an Israeli effort to explore opportunities beyond the present peace process. Israel must gain acceptance as a permanent feature of the Middle East by many of the region's states—including Iran, Iraq, Libya, and the Sudan. Clearly, this would have to be done carefully, without antagonizing the United States—

Israel's most important ally—and states in the region with which Israel maintains or is attempting to establish relations of peace and cooperation—Egypt, Jordan, Saudi Arabia, and the smaller Gulf states.

Coupled with its pursuit of conflict resolution, Israel would need to maintain most facets of its deterrence both as a hedge against possible conflict with any of the peace process states and to dissuade an attack from the remaining rejectionist states—primarily Iraq and Iran. Until all major security threats have been removed, Israel would need to maintain deterrence based on its ambiguous nuclear posture. Such deterrence would serve to dissuade an attack with unconventional weapons by "rogue states"—Iraq and Iran, for example—and provide a hedge against the possibility that one of the region's states might withdraw from global nuclear nonproliferation efforts and clandestinely acquire nuclear weapons with which it might threaten Israel's survival.

In the conventional realm, Israel would be inclined to place even greater emphasis on its offensive military doctrine and force structure. Territorial concessions in the West Bank and Golan Heights—required to reach an accommodation with its Arab neighbors—would remove Israel's limited tactical depth. Should war occur under such circumstances, Israel could not risk fighting on its own territory and would feel an ever greater imperative to "transfer the battle to the adversary's territory."

With regard to force structure, transferring the battle to the adversary's territory would require Israel to maintain its qualitative edge, to continue to emphasize mobility, to maintain the strength of its air force, and to avoid a costly and prolonged war of attrition. For this purpose, Israel would need to maintain the ability to destroy quickly an adversary's command and control facilities, other high-value targets, logistics supply lines, and second- and third-echelon forces.

To compensate for territorial concessions, Israel will have to insist on "defense in depth." Primarily, this refers to warning of an attack well before it starts so that the IDF's reserve units can be mobilized in time. Defense in depth includes the demilitarization of territory, ground-based sensors and early warning stations, the continued development and early deployment of intelligence satellites, aerial surveillance through "open-skies" arrangements, and a multinational team of monitors.

The possible "over-the-horizon" threats of ballistic missiles and other WMD from Iraq and Iran pose a special problem. As already mentioned, Israel would be strongly inclined to maintain its ambiguous nuclear posture to dissuade a WMD attack by one of these states. In addition, Israel would wish to reduce its exposure to such attacks by taking preventive and preemptive action. This might entail the ability to destroy facilities dedicated to the production of nuclear weapons and to destroy ballistic missile launchers in western Iraq. These imperatives would also require delivery systems that can reach Iran, such as the F-15I long-range strike aircraft.

Other activities designed to reduce Israel's exposure are likely to be explored in the realm of active defense. Primarily, Israel is likely to complete the development of and to deploy the "Arrow" antitactical ballistic missile (ATBM) system. Decisions on this matter are likely to be made pragmatically by taking into account the financial resources that would need to be devoted to such deployment and the estimated effectiveness of the system. Any leakage of incoming ballistic missiles would make such a system irrelevant in the event of a nuclear attack, since a single nuclear warhead would be devastating. But even a system that reduced the leakage by only 70 percent would significantly diminish Israel's exposure to ballistic missiles carrying conventional, chemical, or biological warheads.

In addressing these and other threats, Israel would need to strike a new balance between self-reliance and outside assistance. This refers primarily to the importance of increasing strategic cooperation with the United States. The Arrow missile is already a significant facet of such cooperation—about three-quarters of its development costs are financed by the Pentagon's BMDO. Israel may also need U.S. financial help to deploy the system—the missiles and their launchers, ground-based radar, and command and control facilities. Israel also lacks the technological means for obtaining instant warning of missile launchings from a distance of some 1,200–1,300 kilometers. Should progress in Middle East peacemaking lead to an Israeli–Syrian accord, financial pressures will only increase because of the expected costs of redeploying IDF forces and installations from the Golan Heights.

Much more challenging, however, will be the task of adjusting these security imperatives to the new regional peace environment. As long as Israel faced deeply hostile neighbors, it could enhance security through self-help measures and largely ignore the effect on the neighbors' threat perceptions. Now, however, Israeli security measures may elicit an Arab reaction that might shake the foundations of Middle East peacemaking.

This point may be clarified by examining the conceptual problems entailed in Israel's attempts to prepare itself against the over-the-horizon threats presented by Iran and Iraq, as well as in its more general continued quest for effective deterrence. Without mitigating measures, a major Israeli military buildup may be perceived as threatening Israel's neighbors, especially given the "technological jump" required to withstand these more distant adversaries. Israel's neighbors might also fear that Israel might violate their sovereign airspace to prevent attacks from Iran and Iraq. Regardless of the peace agreements, Israel's neighbors are unlikely to ignore a dramatic improvement in Israel's weaponry.

A more general problem involves the ability to maintain deterrence under conditions of peace. Deterrence could enhance peace by dissuading states seeking peace from abandoning the peace process and by deterring rogue states from challenging the peacemakers. At the same time, deterrence implies threats that can harm warm relations and the spirit of accommodation.

This highlights the complex relationship between confidence building, arms control, deterrence, and peace. As noted earlier, confidence building is an important facet of arms control. More secure states are less fearful of exploring possibilities for significant arms reductions. Confidence building also enhances peace since secure states are less likely to feel compelled to take preventive and preemptive action.

At the same time, deterrence cannot be obtained without making states feel less secure. Indeed, the greater the threat, the more robust the deterrent. But this brings us back to the original dilemma: are states lacking self-confidence likely to maintain peace? While Israel would like to be embraced by its Arab neighbors, in attending to its security it seeks to be feared. In the eyes of one Arab observer, "Israel would like to be loved and feared at the same time. It cannot have it both ways."

This dilemma underscores the main point of this section: peace requires Israel to pursue its national security policy with ever greater subtlety and sophistication. Arms control and confidence building should be pursued as an integral part of national security—not at the expense of deterrence. Deterrence should be maintained, but in a more measured and focused manner, so that threats can be deterred without frightening newly acquired friends. In this spirit a new balance will have to be pursued between deterrence and reassurance. This new balance will have to be reflected in all facets of Israel's national security affairs: its grand strategy, military doctrine, force structure, and arms control policy.

3

Arab National Security Issues: Perceptions and Policies

Abdullah Toukan

THE MIDDLE EAST REGIONAL security environment is certainly not struc- tured solely around the Arab-Israeli conflict. Many states in the region have participated in other regional disputes and conflicts. However, since the Palestinian issue is at the heart of the Arab-Israeli conflict, it has re- mained for many years the defining axis around which much of the politics of the Middle East was organized. For over forty-five years of displacement and nonrecognition and twenty-five years of occupation, the threat to the Palestinian people has become one of national existence. As a result, Arab national security thinking evolved primarily from this arena. An attempt to ascertain this thinking comprises the main thrust of this chapter.

The first section attempts to reflect how the Arab states viewed Israel and the threat it posed. It also elaborates the grand strategy that the Arab states have adopted in order to cope with the challenges that Israel pre- sented, and it describes the role of the Gulf and Maghreb states in the Middle East at large. The second section addresses possible opportunities that emerge as a result of the Arab-Israeli peace process and the new re- gional security environment it helped to create. The third section provides an overview of the Arab states' approach to arms control, focusing on the positions that these states have adopted in the Arms Control and Regional Security (ACRS) multilateral talks. The final section analyzes how future Arab security policy might address these changes and developments.

Arab States' Perceptions of Their Security Environment

Over the past five decades the Arab-Israeli conflict—with the struggle of the Palestinian people at its core—absorbed much of the region's energies and resources. The five wars in 1948, 1956, 1967, 1968–70 (war of attrition), and 1973 extracted high tolls in terms of human casualties: 18,600 Arabs (Egyptians, Jordanians, Palestinians, and Syrians) and 8,530 Israelis were killed or wounded.[1]

These wars also resulted in a significant expansion of the territories controlled by Israel, as a consequence of military operations and intrusions, relative to those accorded it by the 1947 UN partition plan. After the 1967 war, Israel occupied the Syrian Golan Heights, the Gaza Strip, the West Bank, and the entire Sinai Peninsula. After invading Lebanon in 1978, Israel also occupied an area of south Lebanon. Jordan also lost territory east of its international boundary with mandated Palestine. These lands fell under Israeli control as a consequence of military operations and intrusions beyond the demarcation line.

The Arab world regarded Israel as the common enemy and viewed it as dangerously aggressive and expansionist, seeking to achieve regional hegemony while pretending to strive for peace. Israel was seen as aiming to prolong its occupation of Arab territory by derailing any opportunity for achieving peace and by irrevocably altering the demographic and geographic realities of the Middle East. These perceptions were later substantiated by former Israeli prime minister Yitzhak Shamir when he revealed his intention to prolong autonomy negotiations for at least ten years. At the same time, Israel planned to settle some half a million Soviet Jewish immigrants in the West Bank and Gaza Strip to make its control irreversible.

Israel was further generally seen as using all means to keep the Middle East unstable and in continuous political turmoil. This perception was

[1]Anthony Cordesman, *The Arab-Israeli Military Balance and the Peace Process. An Analytic Summary of the Balance* (Washington D.C.: Center for Strategic and International Studies, November 6, 1995).

based on the belief that Israel never recognized and respected the Arab rights to sovereignty and territorial integrity. Israel was also viewed as fearing that peace would allow the Arab states to redirect their resources into economic reform and development, which was not in Israel's interests. Consequently, many in the Arab world were convinced that Israel was determined to keep the region in a state of conflict and underdevelopment to dominate the region more easily.

Israel was perceived as deliberately avoiding the demarcation of its borders with the adjacent Arab countries. At most, Israel was seen as willing to negotiate a readjustment of borders to meet its security requirements. Consequently, Israel's declared peaceful intentions were viewed as a means to conclude peace treaties without the linkage between sovereignty and secure borders. Israel was also viewed as a country that—under the pretext that its security was threatened—would invade an Arab neighbor to gain territory and would then claim that the territory was historically disputed. This was the Arab interpretation of the causes and outcomes of the 1956 and 1967 wars. These Israeli actions and statements lay at the heart of the Arabs' threat perception.

In October 1956, the Suez war was started when Israel, allied with France and Britain, attacked Egypt. By the end of the Suez war, Israel had occupied the Sinai and the Gaza Strip. In the aftermath of the war, international pressure—with the United States at the forefront—was exerted on Israel to withdraw from the Sinai and the Gaza Strip promptly and unconditionally. Israel resisted, arguing that the Gaza Strip had been part of mandated Palestine and that Egypt had violated numerous UN Security Council (UNSC) cease-fire resolutions when it invaded the Gaza Strip in 1948 and then used the territory as a springboard for aggression against Israel. The United States cosponsored two UN resolutions, one deploring Israel's noncompliance with the UN General Assembly's repeated demands to withdraw without delay, and the second calling for scrupulous respect for the 1949 Armistice Agreement so that the UN Emergency Force (UNEF) could be interposed to prevent or minimize armed infiltration and reprisals.

At the end of the Suez war, Egypt had allowed UNEF forces on its side of the border with Israel as well as along the eastern coast of the Sinai Peninsula, despite Israel's adamant refusal to permit UNEF forces on its side of the border. This was seen as placing Egypt on unequal terms with its enemy to the east. Nevertheless, UNEF did its best to supervise and maintain the parties' armistice and cease-fire commitments.

In the 1967 war, Israel was viewed by the Arab states as using the pretext that its security was threatened to launch a preemptive air and land attack on Egypt. Jordan, Syria, and Iraq also participated in the war against Israel. Fearing an Israeli attack, Iraq agreed to send troops to Syria, Egypt, and Jordan. Iraq and Egypt signed a defense pact on June 4, and Jordan also signed a defense agreement with Egypt whereby Jordanian military forces were to be placed under Egyptian command. In six days Israeli military forces seized the Sinai Peninsula up to the Suez Canal, the Gaza Strip, the Syrian Golan Heights, and the entire West Bank.

After the 1967 war, the UN Security Council adopted Resolution 242, which the Arab states viewed as providing a plan for resolving the Middle East dispute by stipulating that Israel withdraw from all the territories occupied during the 1967 war. By contrast, Israel regarded the resolution as a statement of principles on the basis of which the parties would negotiate peace. What concerned the Arabs most was that Israel immediately began to develop arguments for annexing or at least maintaining control of the occupied territories for as long as necessary for security reasons. Israel began claiming the right to occupy the territories until a peace treaty ensured safe boundaries. Israel also contended that UNSC Resolution 242 required it "to agree to territorial arrangements only to the extent that doing so would not jeopardize security." Israel claimed that the resolution stipulated that when peace was concluded, it would withdraw to "secure and recognized" boundaries to be determined by a negotiated agreement, and that these boundaries need not be identical to the 1949 armistice demarcation lines.

Arab states interpreted UNSC Resolution 242 as condemning the acquisition of territory by war and demanding that Israel withdraw. Nowhere in the resolution was the withdrawal made conditional on a peace treaty. Resolution 242 did not and could not include a provision according to which Israel could occupy Palestinian territory and hold its people hostage until the Arab states agreed to a peace treaty that defined boundaries meeting Israel's security concerns. Such a condition would be in violation of the basic principles of international law, which cannot be modified by the Security Council or any other body.

Furthermore, the Arab countries contended that Israel acquired no title to the West Bank, the Gaza Strip, or East Jerusalem. Great Britain was granted the League of Nations' mandate for Palestine in 1922, and retained control of the territory until 1947. The League of Nations' mandate did not provide a title to these territories. Instead, it preserved the residual sovereignty of the Palestinian people by promising that when Britain assumed the League of Nations' mandate in Palestine, it would be responsible for putting into effect the Balfour Declaration of November 2, 1917. The declaration stipulates the "establishment in Palestine of a national home for the Jewish people . . . it being clearly understood that nothing should be done which might prejudice the civil and religious rights of existing non-Jewish communities in Palestine, or the rights and political status enjoyed by Jews in any other country." When the British ended their rule and left Palestine in 1947, the mandate was superseded by UNGA Resolution 181(II). Accepted by Israel, the resolution recommended the establishment of an "independent Arab and Jewish State and the Special International Regime for the City of Jerusalem" and described the boundaries of the Arab state, the Jewish state, and Jerusalem.

The occupation continued even after the 1973 war. Arab states were concerned that Israel would continue to separate the issues of sovereignty and secure borders as well as dilute UNSC Resolution 242 of 1967 and 338 of 1973, and attempt to change "occupied territories" into "disputed territories." In this situation the Arab states demanded that there had to be a clear difference between Israeli security requirements and territorial aspirations.

Israel was perceived as pursuing a dual strategy of deterrence and compellence through its superior military capabilities and strategic weapons. In addition, this weaponry was seen as an Israeli warning to the Arab states that they would not be capable of altering the status quo. Therefore, the only alternative Israel left for the Arab states was to recognize Israel and sign an imposed peace treaty with political and security terms dictated by Israel.

Arab Strategic Vulnerability

The dual challenge of Israel's qualitative military advantage, especially in air power, and borders very close to vital Arab civilian and military strategic centers had no easy solution. Strategic depth vulnerability to an Israeli military attack was one of the main concerns of both Jordan and Syria. Both countries have most of their population, industries, food production areas, and main water resources in the west, very close to the borders with Israel.

Damascus is about 40 kilometers from Israeli frontline troops in the Golan Heights and more than 80 percent of Syria's population and industry are concentrated in the west. The threat as seen from Damascus comes from two directions: the Golan Heights and the border with Lebanon, which is only 20 kilometers from Damascus. Syria is concerned that Lebanon could be used as a staging ground for attacks. Of particular concern is the Bekaa valley, which could provide Israeli ground forces with access to the center of Syria.

Among all the Arab countries, Jordan shares the longest borders with Israel. The capital, Amman, is less than 70 kilometers from Israel's pre-1967 borders, and about 90 percent of Jordan's population is less than 50 kilometers away from Israel's borders. The arms race by the surrounding countries, with both conventional and unconventional weapons, as well as the high state of military preparedness, was a threat to Jordan. Building a basic self-defense military capability absorbed a large portion of scarce economic and human resources.

Another threat to Jordan was the Israeli occupation of the West Bank and Gaza. The massive Jewish immigration into Israel and the building of settlements in the occupied territories caused an uncontrollable migration of Palestinians into Jordan, which created political, economic, and security problems. Jordan had already been host to three waves of Palestinian refugees in 1948, after the 1967 war, which increased the population of Jordan by 35 percent, and in 1991, when approximately 350,000 returnees were displaced from the Gulf states as a result of the Gulf War.

Arab countries were disturbed by the public debate in Israel on its "strategic depth vulnerability" to a possible attack from the east, which was claimed to constitute a threat to Israel's national security. It was further argued that the West Bank can provide a "security buffer" against such an attack, and therefore Israel must retain full military and political control. This security buffer argument was seen as another Israeli attempt at justifying its occupation of the West Bank. Israelis maintained this argument until the recent 1991 Gulf War, when surface-to-surface missiles launched by Iraq landed in the heartland of Israel, which deflated the concept of "security buffer."

Nuclear Weapons

For the Arab world, another threat emanates from Israel's nuclear capability and its parallel commitment to prevent Arab nuclearization, even if Arab facilities are for peaceful purposes and comply with safeguards of the International Atomic Energy Agency (IAEA). It has been reported that Israel has one hundred to two hundred nuclear warheads and has produced a number of delivery systems, such as the Jericho-IIB surface-to-surface ballistic missile with a range of 1,450 to 2,500 kilometers.[2]

Israel has repeatedly declared that "it would not be the first country to introduce nuclear weapons in the region," and some Israeli analysts declared that these are "weapons of last resort." The Arab states' view is that such nuclear doctrines can never be considered binding in case of war.

Some Israelis contend that during the Gulf War, their nuclear capability deterred Iraq from fitting chemical or biological warheads in the surface-to-surface missiles launched against Israel. Many in the Arab world believe, however, that the warnings by the coalition forces and the international community deterred Iraq. Former U.S. secretary of state James Baker wrote about his meeting with Tarik Aziz in Geneva a few days before the war broke out, in which he delivered a very strong warning to Iraq on the consequences of using chemical or biological weapons.[3]

This strong U.S. warning certainly did not imply that nuclear weapons would be used against Iraq. The danger would be if analysts interpret the U.S. warning as referring to a nuclear retaliation, and that it was the reason why Saddam Hussein did not use chemical or biological weapons in Kuwait, or against Israel and Saudi Arabia. This kind of interpretation, especially by Israel, could lead to an open-ended prescription for states to justify acquiring or retaining nuclear weapons as a deterrent against perceived biological or chemical threats. The reverse is also possible: States

[2]International Institute for Strategic Studies, London, in its *Military Balance 1995/96* reports that Israel has up to one hundred nuclear warheads, and the Jericho-II ballistic missile (tested in 1987–89) has a range of 1,500 kilometers. See also James Bruce, *Jane's Defense Weekly*, March 25, 1995, "To sign or not to sign: Israel embattled over NPT refusal" says that Israel is estimated to have some two hundred nuclear warheads; Harold Hough, *Jane's Intelligence Review*, November 1, 1994, p. 508, "Israel's Nuclear Infrastructure"; Gerald M. Steinberg, *International Defense Review*, October 1995, "Middle East Space Race Gathers Pace," writes that the Jericho-IIB ballistic missile has a range between 1,450 and 2,800 kilometers.
[3]James A. Baker III, *The Politics of Diplomacy: Revolution, War, and Peace 1989–1992* (New York: G.P. Putnam's Sons, 1995), p. 359.

could justify their interest in biological or chemical weapons to deter nuclear attack. The ultimate objective of many Arab states, in contrast, is to curb the proliferation of weapons of mass destruction in the region and not to encourage proliferation by debating the deterrent effects of the weapons.

From the time the Non-Proliferation Treaty (NPT) was drafted in 1968, Arab states have been calling for Israel to join, but Israel has refused. Western countries secured an indefinite extension of the treaty in April 1995, without Israel becoming a party to the treaty. This led a number of Arab countries to state that selectivity and dual standards regarding disarmament when dealing with the NPT will no doubt stimulate an arms race in the region. By not supporting the Arab states in putting pressure on Israel, Western countries were accused by the Arab states of denying the rights of nonnuclear states to be assured of safety against the nuclear threat surrounding them.

Israeli-U.S. Strategic Relationship

Israel's strategic relationship with the United States and its qualitative military edge were also perceived as a threat by Arab states. To them this relationship gave Israel not only access to advanced weapons and technology for its military industries but also a qualitative military edge far superior to all the Arab defense forces put together.

The "Memorandum of Understanding Between the Government of the United States and the Government of Israel on Strategic Cooperation" of November 30, 1981, outlined the cooperative relationship to deter and contain Soviet threats to the region.[4] This cooperation was in three areas: military assistance for operations of their forces that may be required to cope with this threat, cooperation in research and development, and the positioning of military equipment in Israel that could be used by U.S. military forces. Israel was perceived as having positioned itself as the only reliable U.S. ally in the Middle East that could carry out the U.S. strategy of deterring and containing the Soviet Union.

The Arab states have a continuing concern about Israeli-U.S. cooperation in military research and development, in particular, the Arrow Missile

---

[4]Shai Feldman, "The Future of U.S.-Israel Strategic Cooperation," The Washington Institute for Near East Policy, p. 65.

System. This research and development program has been described as a tactical antiballistic missile defense system costing an estimated $2 billion, of which 72 percent comes from the U.S. Ballistic Missile Defense Organization.[5] The weapon system is supposedly designed to counter the future Arab ballistic missile threat by destroying missiles 100 miles from their target. Associated with this program is the Israeli Ofeq satellite system that will probably be used to detect and locate hostile missile launchers for the Arrow system to intercept.

Arab observers are concerned with reports that the Ofeq can be used as a surveillance satellite flying over Arab countries collecting intelligence information.[6] These reports have generated speculation that Israel has been stalling on the peace talks with Syria until it successfully tests the various components of the system. It is also likely that the Arrow and Ofeq programs will strengthen the Israeli position in negotiations with Syria concerning withdrawal from the Golan Heights. Arab states see Israel's missile and satellite program, in conjunction with its nuclear arsenal and military superiority, as a threatening development in the next few years. Israel will have the capability of launching an attack on any Arab state without the fear of an effective ballistic missile retaliation, a capability that cannot be matched in the region.

Arab States and the Soviet Union

The Arab states as a whole did not conclude any such agreements with the Soviet Union, nor did they intend to deter the United States from the region. Some Arab countries and the Soviet Union had "Agreements of Friendship and Cooperation," such as the Soviet-Syrian agreement in 1980 and earlier agreements with Iraq and the People's Democratic Republic of Yemen. From a Soviet perspective the agreements merely reinforced the international legal basis of their involvement in the region.

The Soviet Union was viewed by the West as taking advantage of the Arab-Israeli conflict to advance its geopolitical goals and to drive the West out of the region. The goals of the Soviet Union were said to be eliminating Western influence, establishing itself as the dominant power in the

[5]Mark Stenhouse, "The Middle East Peace Process—A False Dawn or a New Era?" *International Defense Review-Yearbook*, December 31, 1994, p. 98.
[6]*Jane's Intelligence Review*, September 1, 1995, "Arrow May Upset Middle Eastern Power Balance," p. 8.

region, threatening vital sea routes, outflanking NATO, and gaining a stronghold in the oil-producing countries. Furthermore, according to Western analysts, the active Soviet support for the Arabs after 1955 introduced the Cold War into the Arab-Israeli conflict and the threat of a confrontation between the superpowers.

Other Western analysts maintain that the Cold War brought the Soviet Union into the Middle East and led to its direct support of the Arab states in the Arab-Israeli conflict. They further argue that there was no evidence that the Soviets ever sought to seize Middle East oil or deny the West access to it.

Throughout the five Arab-Israeli wars, the superpowers pursued a dual policy of transferring arms to the region and searching for a peaceful settlement. The Soviet Union and the United States practiced crisis management instead of conflict prevention and avoidance, maintaining the status quo and the regional balance of power and pursuing *détente*.

The Arab Gulf States and Iraq

Outside the Arab-Israeli arena, in the Arabian Peninsula, the members of the Gulf Cooperation Council (GCC) were exposed to a number of threats. In an envisioned conflict between East and West before the end of the Cold War, Western states feared a Soviet invasion to deprive them of Middle Eastern oil. Another perceived external threat was the disruption of shipping lanes in the Bab-el-Mandeb and the Red Sea, through which most oil tankers must pass. To the Gulf states, Israel was the only conceivable threat from the north.

During the 1980s, after the Khomeini revolution in Iran and its belligerent propaganda calling for the overthrow of the Gulf Arab regimes and the establishment of regimes loyal to its Shia revolutionary ideals, Iran became the most immediate threat to Iraq and the Gulf states. Though Iran had the air capability to strike at the GCC states, it was an overland invasion that was considered as the main threat. Iraq was looked upon as the shield of the peninsula from the east, specifically in the Basra region, the only possible route for an Iranian ground invasion. Sovereignty and territorial integrity had become the underlying security concerns for the Gulf states and Iraq. One of the main reasons that Iraq went to war with Iran was to force the new Iranian regime to recognize Iraqi sovereignty over the Shatt al Arab, the river formed by the Tigris and Euphrates rivers in southeast Iraq.

The war enhanced the legitimacy of the Iraqi regime internationally. Iran revealed its ambitions for hegemony over the Gulf and farther afield in the Arab world, and Iraq's struggle became transformed into a defense of the Arab world as a whole from the non-Arab peoples of the east.

The Iran-Iraq war was fought with outdated weapon systems. Air-to-air combat was almost nonexistent, and Iraq enjoyed an overall air superiority. In the opinion of many Western military analysts, Iran's method of attack, using human waves, was very close to that used in World War I. However, as the Iran-Iraq war continued throughout the 1980s, three main types of warfare came to the attention of Western military analysts: attacks on strategic and economic targets (mainly the petrochemical industries and oil tankers), surface-to-surface missiles (SSMs) fired at cities, which later came to be known as the "war of the cities," and the use of chemical weapons.

Iraq learned from the war that it needed a military deterrent to Iranian aggression to compensate for its smaller population. Iraq contained Iran for eight years because of superior weaponry and the economic and military aid it openly received from the West and the Gulf states. The Iraqi leadership was apparently determined to maintain that advantage, which was also seen as the only way of deterring Israeli aggression and as a way for Iraq to project itself as a significant regional power. As a result, military strength was given far higher priority by the Iraqi leadership than economic prosperity. Overriding importance was given to the development of an indigenous armaments industry and the development of weapons of mass destruction and surface-to-surface missiles.

The expressions of concern by Israel and the West were perceived by the Iraqi leadership as efforts to curb Iraq's plans and to undermine its growing power and influence in the region. The initial interpretation of this perceived threat was that the West might encourage Israel to strike Iraq's military facilities in a repeat of its 1981 attack on the Osiraq nuclear reactor.

To deter such an attack, Saddam Hussein described Iraq's plans for massive retaliation in a number of speeches in early 1990. He said, "We will make the fire eat up half of Israel if it tries to strike against Iraq," clearly implying that Iraq would launch chemical weapons at Israel.

The Gulf War

During the Iran-Iraq war, Kuwait and the other GCC countries had fully supported Iraq with substantial economic aid. Once the war was over, Kuwait wanted to finalize the demarcation of its borders with Iraq. However, in addition to economic reasons such as Iraq's accusations that Kuwait was pumping oil from the al-Rumaila fields situated in the disputed border region, and Kuwait's refusal to lease the two islands of Warbah and Bubiyan to Iraq for sea access to the Gulf, Iraq began to claim that Kuwait was part of Iraq, its nineteenth province. With these arguments Iraq then invaded Kuwait in August of 1990.

Immediately following the liberation of Kuwait by the UN coalition led by the United States, the UN Security Council passed Resolution 687, which set the terms of the settlement of the Gulf War. The terms of the resolution also attempted to curb the proliferation of weapons of mass destruction in the Middle East. It called for Iraq to accept unconditionally all actions taken under international supervision for the destruction, removal, or rendering harmless of all chemical and biological weapons, all stocks of agents and related subsystems and components, all research, development, support, and manufacturing facilities, all ballistic missiles with a range greater than 150 kilometers, related major parts and repair and production facilities. The resolution required Iraq to agree unconditionally not to acquire or develop nuclear weapons or nuclear-usable material, any subsystems or components, or any research, development, support, or manufacturing facilities. Many analysts commented that the mandatory intrusive intervention in the internal affairs of Iraq had never been imposed before on a member state of the UN. Many in the Arab world noted that the resolution takes steps toward the goal of establishing in the Middle East a zone free from weapons of mass destruction and all missiles for their delivery. It also moves toward the goal of a global ban on chemical weapons.

The Maghreb States

Even though the Maghreb states (Algeria, Libya, Mauritania, Morocco, and Tunisia) were not directly involved militarily in the Arab–Israeli conflict, their political contributions were substantial. After the Egyptian–Israeli peace treaty in 1979, with the exclusion of Egypt from Arab League activities, the league's headquarters were moved to Tunis. Following the Israeli invasion of Lebanon in 1982, the Palestine Liberation Organization (PLO) also moved its headquarters to Tunis. Morocco has hosted a number of Arab League summit meetings. Algeria was involved in negotiations to free the U.S. embassy staff members taken hostage in Tehran in 1979.

Algeria has been accused of pursuing a nuclear program and of seeking to construct a nuclear bomb with the assistance of China and Iran. Algeria has since then signed the nuclear Non-Proliferation Treaty and has opened all its facilities to inspections by the IAEA. Libya's chemical weapons capability has been widely acknowledged in the West. Libya's attempts to develop nuclear weapons are reportedly unsuccessful, however.[7] Libya is currently subject to UN sanctions imposed in 1992 after it failed to hand over two Libyans accused in the United States and the UK of planting a bomb on the Pan American airliner that exploded over Lockerbie, Scotland, in 1988.

The Maghreb states have been preoccupied with their own internal problems and disputes. Much of their resources has been absorbed in dealing with the disputes, but none of these disputes has resulted in all-out war. The Algerian-Moroccan desert war of 1963 and the Libyan-Tunisian conflict of 1980, were relatively short. However, the most enduring conflict in the region has been the struggle for the control of the Western Sahara.

In general, the political and social stability of the Maghreb states was threatened by the rapid growth of the region's population. Decline in the domestic economies of the Maghreb states made them unable to absorb a rapidly increasing and predominantly youthful labor force. This surplus of cheap and unskilled labor was channeled mainly to Western Europe. The Maghreb countries encouraged labor migration as a source of foreign income. Until the mid-1980s, the remittances of overseas workers constituted one of the largest foreign revenue sources.

Large-scale political and economic unrest in the Maghreb states was generating an uncontrollable flow of refugees across the Mediterranean. This vast uncontrolled migration into Europe was perceived as a potential threat to the southern European countries. These countries began seeing the security of their southern flank as being dependent on the political

---

[7]Both the Algerian and Libyan programs have been reported in Mark Stenhouse, "Proliferation and the North-South Divide: The Prospects for Arms Control," *International Defense Review-Yearbook*, December 31, 1994, p. 131.

and economic stability of North Africa. The European perception of the emerging threat from North African states was not military in nature but basically social, economic, and cultural.

Arab Grand Strategy

Since Israel's creation, Arab leaders have called for the restoration of the national inalienable rights of the Palestinian people, including their right to repatriation and self-determination, the establishment of a Palestinian state on Palestinian land, and the liberation of the Arab city of Jerusalem. Arab leaders also resolved to affirm the right of the Palestinian people to establish an independent national authority under the command of the PLO—the sole legitimate representative of the Palestinian people—on any liberated Palestinian territory. Once established, this authority was promised the support of the Arab states in all areas and at all levels and equal representation in any peace talks with Israel.

Arab states supported Palestinian resistance against Israel, most notably in the Intifada. After twenty years of military occupation of the West Bank and Gaza, Palestinian youths rebelled in December of 1987 not with arms but with stones against Israeli oppression, persecution, and deprivation of human rights. The Intifada attracted international attention and despite the brutality of Israeli efforts to crush the uprising, it grew and matured and broadened to encompass many other forms of resistance. In the years that followed, Arab states increased their political and financial support to the Intifada to keep pressure on Israel from within the occupied territories.

To the Arab states, Zionism and the state of Israel constituted a military, economic, and cultural threat to all Arab people. Israel was considered as a threat to the Arab world at large—extending beyond the states whose territory Israel occupies. Arab heads of state, meeting in 1964, declared that the threat placed an obligation on all Arab countries to use all available political and economic resources to confront Israel, and if these means failed, to resort to military measures. The heads of state emphasized the diversion of Jordan River water as an important facet of the Israeli threat. In later summit meetings the Arab heads of state reiterated their commitment to support the states adjacent to Israel and strengthen their militaries to liberate the Arab territories occupied by Israel. Indeed, Arab leaders were resolved that no Arab state should disassociate itself from its obligation, that any comprehensive peace negotiation could not be conducted from a position of weakness, and that no solution should be imposed on the Arab world.

The military and security obligations of Arab states toward each other were based on the Pact of the League of Arab States and Article II of the Joint Defense Agreement. (The Arab League currently consists of twenty-two countries: Algeria, Bahrain, Comoros, Djibouti, Egypt, Iraq, Jordan, Kuwait, Lebanon, Libya, Mauritania, Morocco, Palestine, Oman, Qatar, Saudi Arabia, Somalia, Sudan, Syria, Tunisia, United Arab Emirates, and Yemen.) The agreement states that "the convening states consider any armed attack on any state or states or on forces of the states as an attack on all the states. Thus, in accordance with the right of legal self-defense, the states must aid the attacked state or states and must immediately, unilaterally or collectively, take the necessary steps and use all their resources and means, including the use of their armed forces, to repulse the aggression and restore peace and security."

Responding to Israel's Strategic Advantage

Israel's nuclear capability and ambiguous nuclear policy are still considered by Arab states as major destabilizing factors in the Middle East and a driving force for the proliferation of nuclear weapons and other weapons of mass destruction. This strategic capability drove a number of regional Arab states to declare that some form of an "in-kind" deterrence should be developed or acquired. As a result, some Arab states resorted to a poor nation's atomic bombs; chemical and biological weapons.

Israel's strategic capabilities and qualitative edge, especially in air power, were seen as an effort to monopolize strategic deterrence and dominate the Arab world. In response, some Arab countries accelerated their acquisition of surface-to-surface missiles as well as chemical and biological weapons. With these missiles, some Arab countries could strike Israel from areas beyond the range of Israel's air force.

Arab states adopted a policy of "diversification of arms supplies" to reduce their vulnerability to supply cutoffs and embargoes. Since the 1980s, Egypt, Jordan, and the GCC states have procured weapons from different sources to avoid becoming completely reliant on one supplier nation. Only Iraq and Syria have been completely dependent on Soviet weapons systems. Even though Arab states prefer U.S. weapons, they have bought from other sources on the occasions when they have been thwarted by the U.S. Congress. Jordan, for example, tried to obtain a package of F-16 advanced fighter aircraft and other equipment throughout the 1980s but, when denied by the U.S. Congress, turned to the Soviet Union, France, and Britain. In the early 1980s the U.S. administration decided to sell Airborne Warning and Control System (AWACS) aircraft to Saudi Arabia. Israel and its supporters in the U.S. made an all-out fight against the sale. Only after President Reagan personally intervened did Congress approve the sale. After the 1991 Gulf War, Saudi Arabia tried to acquire F-15Es optimized for ground attack, but the U.S. Congress delayed the export of these systems.

Countries that had access to U.S. technologies were suspicious, however, that Israel had access to specifications and performance data for the same equipment. Many Arab military analysts feared that Israel could develop countermeasures to render their U.S. weapons ineffective in times of war.

The United States has approved sales of equipment to Arab states as long as it is different from equipment going to Israel. After the Gulf War, for example, the U.S. Congress approved a sale of F-15S fighters to Saudi Arabia on the condition that they not be of the same type as those bound for Israel. It has been reported that the F-15 Strike Eagle fighter aircraft bound for Israel will have a technological edge over the Saudi F-15s.[8] This is in line with the U.S. policy of maintaining Israel's qualitative edge over Arab countries.

In 1980 Arab heads of state, meeting at a summit in Jordan, agreed that they must attain "strategic parity" with Israel. In addition they endorsed the establishment of a joint Arab military command, with the committee of the Joint Arab Defense Agreement in charge of forming it. The establishment of an Arab Organization for Military Industries was also proposed to replace the Arab Organization for Industry (AOI) that was established in Egypt in 1975. Initial consultations took place, however, none of the proposals was ever carried out.

Generally speaking, each Arab country had its own military doctrine and principles of warfare. They were developed to negate the Israeli military doctrine that any war with the Arab states should be a short and decisive

[8]Barbara Starr, "Israel's F-15I will have edge over Saudi 'S,'" *Jane's Defense Weekly*, February 5, 1994, p. 3.

one and that major battles should be fought on Arab territory. Some states, however, had neither the manpower nor the financial resources to achieve strategic parity with Israel. Jordan, for instance, based its military doctrine on war prevention and basic self-defense. On many occasions, to fulfill its obligations based on the Arab League defense pact, it had reallocated limited resources to its defense forces. Israel's doctrine was challenged mainly by Egypt in 1968 and 1973.

In 1968 Egypt launched a war of attrition with artillery bombardments of Israeli positions along the Suez Canal. Israel retaliated with an artillery bombardment and began to fortify its positions along the front. This form of warfare compelled Israeli forces to engage Egyptian forces along static defense lines. In 1970 a cease-fire sponsored by the United States and the Soviet Union ended the fighting. In October 1973 Egypt and Syria launched a surprise attack on Israel. Jordan and Iraq joined the war, fighting alongside Syria's forces in the Golan Heights. This was the first conventional war that Israel did not initiate with a preemptive attack.

The primary objectives of these wars were not military but rather to create a new diplomatic situation. Egypt and Syria hoped that the unacceptable status quo could be changed and thereby allow them to negotiate the recovery of the Sinai and the Golan Heights and, beyond this, to extract a solution to the Palestinian problem. Syria set its national security objectives to regain the Golan Heights. This was pursued within the context of an alliance/partnership with Egypt during the 1973 war. This partnership continued up to 1979 when Egypt concluded the Camp David peace treaty with Israel.

This campaign negated the Israeli operational military doctrine of a "swift and decisive resolution of war" and the concept of "defensible borders," developed after the 1967 war. Apparently, as many Israeli analysts contend, the territories occupied in 1967 gave Israel more strategic depth and created borders that could be defended without resorting to preemptive attacks. In addition the latter part of the war demonstrated that Israeli military strength alone could not bring a political settlement to the conflict by making the Arab states accept the status quo and blocking them from changing the status quo militarily or politically.

The 1973 war also demonstrated that the Arab armies had become more operationally effective in carrying out limited political objectives. The strategic and tactical consequences of the 1973 war were the Egyptian and Syrian surprise attacks on the Bar Lev Line and the Golan lines as a result of careful planning and deception. The most important strategic result of the war was the accomplishment of the Egyptian objective of ending the "no peace, no war" situation with Israel.

The Oil Embargo

After the 1967 war, Arab states decided that an oil embargo was a way to pressure the world and especially the United States to demand that Israel withdraw from the occupied territories. After studying the matter in 1967, however, the Arab League summit conference in September of 1967 abandoned the idea because oil revenues strengthen the economies of Arab states directly affected by Israeli aggression and can serve Arab goals. Just after the 1973 war, however, the decision was reversed and Arab states used oil for the first time to achieve strategic objectives. In an effort to get the United States to put pressure on Israel to accept a cease-fire and to withdraw its military forces to Israel's borders before the 1967 war, Arab oil-producing countries announced an embargo of oil to the United States and a decrease in oil production that dramatically increased oil prices worldwide. The embargo apparently produced a shift in U.S. policy, whereby a peaceful settlement of the Arab-Israeli conflict became a top priority for the Nixon administration.

Arab oil-producing countries, in particular Saudi Arabia, made the lifting of the oil embargo conditional on the disengagement of forces on both the Syrian-Israeli and Egyptian-Israeli fronts. The oil embargo continued until March 1974 when several agreements were signed between Israel and Syria and between Egypt and Israel relating to separation of forces as well as restrictions on the size of forces and equipment in specified zones. They also included verification regimes and control measures to ensure both their execution and their long-term maintenance, as well as the stationing of the United Nations Disengagement Observer Force (UNDOF) to police the cease-fire lines.

Camp David Accords

The Egyptian-Israeli peace treaty had not only defined the international boundaries between the two countries, and reduced the possibility of a military confrontation, but it also enhanced U.S.-Egyptian relations. The United States had become the principal guarantor of the Egyptian-Israeli security relationship. From the military perspective, the Arab world viewed the peace treaty as allowing Israel to free a large number of its forces from the Egyptian front and redeploy them on the Jordanian, Lebanese, and Syrian fronts. This led Syria to view itself as the sole Arab state that could maintain a balance of power with Israel and as a major player in the region's geopolitics. Consequently, Syria formulated its own doctrine of "strategic parity," which called for strengthening the military, economic, and human resources to withstand a war with Israel and counter its qualitative advantage.

War in Lebanon

To many, the war in Lebanon clearly highlighted the fact that Syria had a long way to go in achieving "strategic parity" with Israel, mainly due to inferior Soviet weapons and training. About one hundred Syrian MiG-21 and MiG-23 aircraft were downed in air-to-air combat against Israeli F-15s and F-16s, while Israel lost only three aircraft. The Israeli Defense Forces demonstrated their ability to use modern weapons systems and to control engagements—picking the time and place to fight rather than fighting under the adversaries' rules.

It has been reported that after the war in Lebanon, Syria revised its strategy toward Israel. Rather than pursuing only "strategic parity," the goal became to complement it with "strategic deterrence" to discourage Israel from initiating an attack. If deterrence failed, then Israel was to realize that it would pay a high price in both resources and casualties because Syria would turn the conflict into a costly and prolonged war of attrition, unlike the previous quick and decisive Arab-Israeli wars.

Economic and Diplomatic Isolation of Israel

Arab states have tried to isolate Israel diplomatically and economically. The Arab League has conducted an economic boycott of Israel since 1948. Any direct Arab-Israeli business contacts were forbidden. The boycott also applied to foreign firms that have branches in Israel or do business with Israel. The Arab League member states considered this boycott a legitimate tool that other states and international organizations use.

The Arab states requested support for the boycott from Islamic and Non-Aligned Movement (NAM) countries, the European Community, and several Asian countries. The Soviet Union and Eastern European countries were requested to continue their support for the Palestinian cause and to continue providing military equipment to some of the Arab states. In the UN, the Arab states agreed to coordinate their efforts to isolate Israel and expose its abuses.

With regard to the United States, the Arab states agreed to exert every effort to change the U.S. policy biased in favor of Israel and against the Palestinian people's inalienable national rights, and to warn the United States that its policy would affect its strategic interests in the region. U.S. policy toward Israel was seen as encouraging Israel to continue its aggression and violations of human rights in the occupied territories, which hampered the efforts to achieve peace. As a permanent member of the UN Security Council, the United States was also seen as not fulfilling its responsibilities for the preservation of international peace and security.

The Gulf States

The GCC defense agreements have exposed the Gulf states to a wider spectrum of threats. Stemming from the text of the GCC defense pact, which states that "an attack on one member country would be viewed as an attack on all," a doctrine against external threats was agreed upon containing the principle of "self-reliance" at its core. This principle puts the responsibility for the security of the region on the member states of the GCC.

Following the 1967 and 1973 Arab-Israeli wars and the 1980–89 Iran-Iraq War, the GCC countries decided to build forces that would be strong enough to deter any regional power wanting to occupy and disrupt the oil resources of the Gulf region. Based on this doctrine the Gulf states then initiated extensive programs on defense cooperation and individual arms procurement as well as force structure modernization.

The GCC member states sought alliance agreements with Western powers to enhance their deterrence. This policy helped them to buy advanced weapons from the West. It is the view of some analysts that these alliance agreements, especially between Saudi Arabia and the United States, spared Saudi Arabia from a military confrontation with Israel.

Advanced weapons and alliances with Western powers were seen as the only means to compensate for the Gulf states' deficiency in both military firepower and manpower. Until the mid-1980s, defense expenditures of the Gulf states concentrated mainly on developing infrastructure, and over the last decade priority was given to the acquisition of modern weapons.

The New Regional Security Environment

The new regional security environment that has emerged in the Middle East is a product of the end of the Cold War and the Middle East peace process. The end of the Cold War has removed superpower competition as a destabilizing factor. In the new environment, the superpowers are seen as cooperating with each other as well as with extraregional countries to promote peace and stability in the region.

The Middle East process, cosponsored by the United States and Russia and launched at the October 1991 international conference in Madrid, is seen as providing a bilateral and multilateral framework in which the basic issues that will bring about a comprehensive peace to the Arab-Israeli conflict will be addressed. The peace process is seen as providing the region with the opportunity to establish a broad security framework for the various steps toward achieving arms control and regional security.

Furthermore, military analysts contend that instability in any one of the GCC states or military aggression on a state could easily trigger instability in another Gulf state as well as in the region. The Iran-Iraq War and the recent Gulf War are examples. The security of GCC member states has also been affected by the Arab-Israeli conflict and the struggle of the Palestinian people.

Oslo Agreements

To many in the Arab world the Oslo agreements in 1993 and the Palestinian National Council elections in 1996 marked the end of the Zionist dream of a "Greater Israel." The Oslo-II agreement extended Palestinian self-rule beyond Gaza and Jericho to most of the West Bank and stipulated the redeployment of Israeli military forces outside populated areas. In December 1995 Israel completed the transfer of six West Bank towns to Palestinian control, and on January 20, 1996, Palestinians in the West Bank and Gaza voted for an eighty-eight–member Palestinian National Council and elected PLO chairman Yasir Arafat president of an interim government. The Palestinians were applauded by the international community

on the free and fair elections as well as on the outcome of the elections. As
U.S. officials put it, the elections produced a "mandate for peace" in the
Palestinian community.[9] Following the January 1996 meeting of the Palestinian National Council, Israeli-Palestinian final status negotiations were
set to begin in mid-1996 and to last for three years. These negotiations
were designed to cover final borders, Jerusalem, refugees, security arrangements, and Israeli settlements.

These developments have alleviated Arab states' concern regarding Israel's expansionist policies, which to them lay at the core of Israel's politics
since its creation. The agreements also lay the groundwork for a sovereign
Palestinian state.

Bilateral Negotiations

Negotiations between Syria and Israel regarding security arrangements,
pending a total Israeli withdrawal from the Golan Heights, are under way.
Syria has declared that its objectives are the full implementation of UNSC
Resolutions 242/338 and the evacuation and dismantling of all Israeli settlements—about thirteen thousand settlers in forty-two settlements. Syria
insists that any final security arrangements must guarantee its sovereignty
and be balanced on both sides of the border. According to a number of
reports, Syria does not rule out the possibility of establishing demilitarized
zones and early warning stations on the Golan Heights on both sides of
the border. Syria is unlikely to accept extending the demilitarized zone
beyond the Golan Heights, however. Such a zone could include Damascus
since it is only 40 kilometers away from the Golan Heights, and this could
put the capital in jeopardy.

Syria was generously rewarded by the Gulf states for its participation in
the 1991 Gulf War. The financial assistance from the Gulf states and the
resumption of defense links with Russia have enabled Syria to strengthen
its armed forces. It was reported that in 1994 Russia agreed to forgive
Syria's $10 billion debt for military equipment incurred before the collapse
of the Soviet Union.[10] Russia had also agreed to sell Syria a limited amount
of weapons for self-defense worth an estimated $500 million. For Syria

[9]Reuters World Service, January 22, 1996.
[10]Mark Stenhouse, "Proliferation and the North-South Divide: The Prospects for Arms Control," *International Defense Review-Yearbook*, December 31, 1994, p. 131. See also James
Bruce, "Land of Crisis and Upheaval," *Jane's Defense Weekly*, July 3, 1994, p. 23.

the weapons were essential to counter Israel's military buildup and technological edge. Egypt also benefited considerably from U.S. and Gulf financial aid. The United States canceled $6.7 billion in military debts, and the
Gulf states canceled $7.1 billion in debts.[11]

Lebanon's objectives are the full implementation of UNSC Resolution
425, which calls for the withdrawal of all Israeli forces from south Lebanon. Lebanon also aims to disband and disarm all irregular forces to ensure
that its territories are not used to threaten neighboring states. Israel regards the military operations of the Hezbullah forces in the Israeli self-
declared "security zone" in south Lebanon as terrorist activities. Lebanese
officials, however, have repeatedly stated that these operations are a result
of the Israeli occupation of south Lebanon and are directed at Israeli or
Israeli-related targets in south Lebanon rather than at Israel itself. Prime
Minister Rafik Hariri has said that the Hezbullah forces would only be
disarmed after Israel's withdrawal from Lebanese territory and the full implementation of Resolution 425.

It is too early to assess the ongoing bilateral negotiations. But it is clear
from all official statements that the stakes are too high in terms of damage
to the region for the process to be reversed. A number of Arab analysts
have expressed their fear that with the Likud party in power after the May
1996 elections in Israel, it would pursue the declared policy, which is to
grant the Palestinians more autonomy to administer their daily affairs in
the populated areas of the West Bank and Gaza Strip, but Israel would
maintain sovereignty and full security responsibility for the entire West
Bank and parts of the Gaza Strip. Such a policy implies that the Likud
government would suspend negotiations with the Palestinian Authority
(PA) on issues pertaining to Jerusalem, refugees, and settlements, leaving
local administration as the only issue for negotiation. This certainly would
result in a total breakdown of the peace process and would have a negative
impact on the already concluded peace treaties between Jordan and Israel,
and Egypt and Israel. A breakdown of the peace process would also occur,
if in negotiations with Syria and Lebanon, Israel focuses solely on security
arrangements with no reference to any withdrawal from the Golan
Heights and south Lebanon. Other Arab analysts maintain that the peace
process has been successful and, regardless of what type of Israeli govern-

---

[11]Andrew Rathmell, "Egypt's Military-Industrial Complex," *Jane's Intelligence Review*, October 1, 1994, p. 455. See also David C. Isby, "Continuity and Change in the Egyptian Defense
Industry," *Jane's Intelligence Review-Yearbook*, December 31, 1994, p. 66.

ment is in power, the peace process is irreversible and the government will have to honor all agreements with the PA and Arab states, and resume negotiations with the PA, Syria, and Lebanon.

An Arab heads-of-states summit took place in Cairo on June 23, 1996. The objective of the meeting was to reaffirm the Arab states' commitment to the Middle East peace process, which is based on UN Security Council Resolutions 242 and 338, and the principle of land for peace as stated in the Middle East Peace Conference that started in Madrid on October 30, 1991.[12] They also called for the resumption of peace talks on all tracks.

Changing Military Doctrines

Throughout the history of the Arab-Israeli conflict, two main considerations underlying the choice of a military doctrine have been balance of forces and strategic depth. Lack of strategic depth resulted in limitations on the area of operational maneuverability during war as well as the vulnerability of vital strategic centers due to their proximity to the borders.

As the peace process approaches comprehensive peace, these considerations should be included in the peace treaties. For instance, after Israel withdraws to the pre-1967 internationally recognized borders, both sides will have agreed to establish security arrangements on the international borders, demilitarized zones, and early warning stations. Moreover, all countries will have agreed to certain air and land confidence- and security-building measures (CSBMs) between the military forces in areas around the international boundaries. These security arrangements and CSBMs between the parties should increase transparency, protect against any surprise attack, and put a constraint on the tactical operational military capabilities and activities of the armed forces. These should contribute to the transformation from offensive to more defensive military doctrines and force structure postures.

Many in the Arab world maintain that in the present transition phase, Israel, as a sign of confidence building, should start showing some change in its military doctrine and force structure posture. Any change in Israel's

---

[12]"Inter-Arab: 'Final Communique' Issued by Arab Summit," *FBIS Daily Report: Near East and South Asia*, June 24, 1996, p. 13. On the Madrid conference see: President George Bush, "Address before the Opening Session of the Middle East Peace Conference, Madrid, October 30, 1991," U.S. Department of State Bureau of Public Affairs, *Dispatch Supplement*, "The Middle East Process," February 1992, Vol. 3, Supplement No. 2.

military doctrine would imply a change in its national security policy and grand strategy.

Deterrence has taken two main forms: deterrence by the use of force or the threat to use force, and deterrence by alliances. With comprehensive peace, Arab states and Israel will have agreed that neither side will enter into any new defense alliances that may threaten the security of the other. This would eliminate the threat of an Arab coalition against Israel, which apparently has been a fundamental concern to Israel. On the other hand, Arab states ask why Israel maintains a massive and sophisticated military that gives it a qualitative edge as well as a strategic deterrence capability. From the point of view of the Arab states, Israel has not taken initial steps to change its force structure.

Arab states have come to realize that it is highly unlikely that Israel will discuss strategic deterrence and nuclear weapons in bilateral talks, beyond just declaratory statements of concern. Arab states have been attempting to address these issues in the multilateral ACRS working group forum.

Some analysts observe that for the near future stability and security cannot be based on security arrangements and arms control agreements alone. What they expect to see is an "armed peace" supported by a continued arms race. They claim that there still exists a perception among states in the region that military force is a means to achieve national policy objectives. For this very reason, many states in the region maintain that they should retain their military capabilities until regional peace beyond the Arab-Israeli arena is fully established.

The Gulf States

The Gulf War did not eliminate all possible threats to the Gulf region. Some analysts maintain that the Gulf states are still exposed to external threats from Iran and Iraq even though they are currently subject to a U.S. dual containment policy.

During the Iran-Iraq war, the United States pursued a balance-of-power strategy in the hope that both parties would exhaust each other. In the later part of the war, however, the United States and other Western countries increased their support to Iraq, which finally led to the defeat of Iran. After the Iraqi defeat in the 1991 Gulf War, the United States believed that a balance of power had been achieved between Iran and Iraq at a much lower level of military strength than before. With the steady relative growth of Iranian military strength after 1991, a balance-of-power strategy would have required supporting Iraq once again. The United States has made it clear, however, that it cannot support Iraq as long as Saddam Hussein is in power; hence, the dual containment policy.

U.S. containment policy toward Iraq is tougher than that toward Iran. Its objective toward Iraq is one of containment and overthrow of Saddam, while the objective of the policy toward Iran is one of containment and moderation of its policies. Iraq, unlike Iran, has been undergoing a disarmament program under the supervision of the UN since 1991.

Apparently, eliminating weapons of mass destruction and long-range surface-to-surface missiles from Iraq has not been without problems. The UN commission is periodically revealing evidence of Iraq's noncompliance with the UN resolutions. In December 1995, for example, a shipment of gyroscopes used in the inertial navigational system of long-range ballistic missiles was intercepted in Jordan. The shipment violates UN sanctions against Iraq and has been taken by the international community as an indication that the regime is still attempting to produce medium- to long-range ballistic missiles. As a result, the credibility of the Iraqi leadership and its cooperation with the international community has suffered tremendously.

Some countries in the region, for example, Jordan, see the political situation in Iraq rapidly deteriorating and Iraq's disintegration highly possible in the very near future. Iraq is divided into three zones, two of which are monitored by coalition aircraft: the air exclusion zone over the Shia region south of the 33rd parallel, and the Kurdish "safe haven" north of the 36th parallel. Only the zone between the two parallels is under the control of the central government. Arab governments want an end to the tragedy and suffering of the Iraqi people as soon as possible and the preservation of the country's sovereignty and territorial integrity. Regarding the federation among the three main sectors of Iraqi society—Shiites, Kurds, and Sunnis—this could be an option that the Iraqis might consider in determining the political future of their country, an option that has been proposed by Iraqi opposition leaders. The ultimate objective would be the establishment of a democratic, open, and more-representative government in Iraq.

Some Arab analysts believe that the dual containment policy will not reduce threats to instability in the Gulf region, but, on the contrary, it could increase cooperation between Iran and Iraq and possibly create a bigger threat. They further maintain that Iran and Iraq should be looked upon as potential security partners rather than military threats. In the case of Iran, Europeans suggest that a form of "critical dialogue" should be started in the hope that Iran could be persuaded to accept the Middle East peace process and to moderate its views toward the region.

As for Iraq, Arab states sympathize with the hardships that the Iraqi people are enduring and see a need to end them, but they blame Saddam Hussein for the current situation. Arab states have proposed a slow lifting of the UN sanctions, such as the plan outlined in Security Council Resolution 986 of April 1995, in which the UN and Iraq negotiated the sale of $1 billion of oil every ninety days to buy much-needed food and medicine. Some of the money will also go toward paying war reparations to Kuwait and for the funding of the UN special commission monitoring operations in Iraq.

Other Western analysts justify the dual containment policy because of the rivalry between Iran and Iraq for regional power. They state that with the defeat of Iraq, Iran now sees new opportunities to enhance its strategic interests and to reemerge as the key power in the Gulf region. They have enumerated five threats to the region posed by Iran: Iran's ambition to acquire nuclear weapons and long-range ballistic missiles, its support for international terrorism, its opposition to the Middle East peace process, its offensive conventional military buildup, and its threat to the stability of the Gulf states.

As a response to these threats, the U.S. policy objective in the Gulf is not to allow the area to be dominated by a hegemonic Iran or Iraq. The United States believes that neither country can dominate the Gulf region as long as U.S. military power remains there. The United States maintains that positioning heavy weapons and military supplies in the Gulf states will allow rapid deployment of forces in the event that Iraq once again poses a threat.

Iran opposes the Western military buildup and suspects that on the pretext of a possible Iraqi threat, the United States is actually positioning itself to confront Iran. To many Arab and Western observers, Iran's recent naval buildup is offensively oriented, as shown by the acquisition of Russian Kilo class attack submarines and Chinese missile boats. Iran has also annexed the tiny island of Abu Musa, which dominates the entrance to the Straits of Hormuz. These events have been considered signals of renewed expansionist interest in the region. Iran, however, justifies its rearmament program as solely designed to restore its defensive capabilities. Iran has a

2,440-kilometer coastline along the Persian Gulf and Arabian Sea, which is its only route to export oil, and around 95 percent of its foreign exchange revenue comes from oil export. Thus, naval power has been given a priority in defense policy. Furthermore, Iran still considers itself a regional power, and its rearmament programs are designed to enable it to play a leading role in any Gulf regional security arrangements. For these reasons Iran would like to keep the waters free from any foreign military presence and prevent outside countries from playing a role in shaping the future political characteristics of the Gulf region.

Since 1991 the Gulf states have invested heavily in the modernization and upgrading of their military capabilities. After the Gulf War, the GCC countries accelerated the modernization of their force structure. The United States, France, and United Kingdom have been the major weapons suppliers. Western military analysts believe that despite the massive arms acquisitions, the Gulf countries could not defend themselves against a massive assault by Iran or Iraq. The active military manpower of the GCC member states is estimated to be 225,000, while that of Iran is around 500,000, and of Iraq, 400,000.[13] The GCC member states also recognize that for some time the assistance of outside regional powers will be required to deal with any military aggression in the region. As a result, they have signed bilateral defense agreements with their Western allies— Britain, France, and the United States.

The 1991 Damascus Declaration called for security cooperation between the GCC and its two main Arab allies, Egypt and Syria, by keeping their troops in the Gulf region after the war. The declaration has not been implemented, however, because the GCC states would prefer to develop their own force structures rather than rely on and financially support foreign or Arab troops on their territory. Consequently, Egypt and Syria have withdrawn their military forces.

Despite the increased security cooperation and defense coordination among GCC member states, tension still exists on territorial matters and demarcation of their common borders. Land and sea boundaries have been unclear for over half a century following the departure of the British. Most have been resolved peacefully, but some have turned into armed clashes, for example, the Qatari-Saudi border clashes in 1992 and again in 1994.

[13]*The Military Balance 1995–96* (Oxford: International Institute for Strategic Studies, 1996), pp. 138–150.

Outside of the GCC member states, Saudi Arabia and Yemen are negotiating differences in the demarcation of their 1,500-kilometer border that led to military clashes in December 1994 and January 1995.

Regional Implications of the Peace Process

Many Western analysts contend that the Arab-Israeli peace process is likely to affect the regional roles of both Iraq and Iran. As the Arab states directly negotiating with Israel are ending their state of hostility, Iran and Iraq are being diplomatically bypassed and regionally isolated. Iran, in particular, has been unable to have any influence on the pace and direction of the peace process.

It is thought that if Lebanon and Syria both sign a peace treaty with Israel, then the long-standing Iranian-Syrian limited alliance may be effectively terminated. This, they maintain, could be a severe setback to Iran, since it considers Syria to be its only regional ally. Israeli-Syrian peace could also severely reduce Iran's access to and influence on the Hezbullah in Lebanon.

A comprehensive peace could then enable the Gulf states to sign their own peace treaties with Israel, thereby completing Iran's isolation in the region. The isolation of Iran could very well convince its leadership that the only pragmatic policy is to recognize the peace treaties between the Arab states and Israel. Subsequently, negotiations among the Arab states, Israel, and Iran on security and cooperation could be started.

Approaches to Arms Control

Attempts to introduce arms control agreements in the Middle East are not new. Over the past four decades several arms control proposals have been put forward: the tripartite (France, UK, and United States) declaration in 1950 to limit arms to the region, the proposal for a nuclear weapon–free zone (NWFZ) first put forward in 1974 in the UN General Assembly by Egypt and Iran, and the U.S. arms control initiative begun in March 1991. The latest U.S. proposals called for a freeze on new surface-to-surface missiles in the region, a halt in the production of nuclear, biological, and chemical weapons, and a new effort by nations that supply conventional weapons to limit supplies.

Two main limitations to these proposals were the Cold War and the absence of a political process such as the current Middle East peace process. The Arab-Israeli conflict made it practically impossible to initiate any formal arms control negotiations in the region. Negotiations on arms control and regional security in the Middle East had to be linked with a peace process.

With regard to conventional weapons, the Arab states are concerned about Israeli statements calling for a conference of Middle Eastern countries with states that supply them arms.[14] This proposal is looked upon as an attempt by Israel to control conventional arms, the only area in which Arab states can compete with Israel, by limiting external sources. It is believed that such an approach would benefit Israel because it produces many of its own weapons, including missiles and tanks, while Arab states rely heavily on foreign supplies.

It has become apparent to many in the Arab countries that are involved in the ACRS process, that Israel favors a structural arms control process focusing on conventional weapons first and separately without any link to unconventional arms control. In contrast, Arab states demand that structural arms control should initially deal with unconventional weapons because of Israel's reported possession of one hundred to two hundred nuclear weapons and advanced surface-to-surface missiles.

Bilateral and Multilateral Levels of Arms Control

It has become quite evident that the interrelation between conflicts and disputes in the Middle East region, coupled with sophisticated weapons that give states strategic striking capability, have highlighted and reinforced the security linkages between states in the region. Within the context of arms control and proliferation, in particular weapons of mass destruction and their delivery systems, each state's threat perception on a bilateral and regional level has become one of the determining factors of its own definition of the Middle East region and its national security objectives, military doctrine, and force structure.

For these reasons it is essential that arms control and transparency measures be pursued at both bilateral and multilateral levels that are comple-

---

[14]Jackson Diehl, "Israel Seeks Conference to Limit Mideast Arms; Conventional Weapons Suppliers Are Target," *Washington Post*, May 28, 1991, p. A15.

mentary to each other. Arms control can be central to the entire process because it could provide the means to translate the political breakthroughs into long-term military stability. At the same time, arms control can reinforce the political breakthroughs by promoting dialogue and trust between the parties.

One approach to addressing conventional and unconventional weapons on a bilateral level leading to a multilateral level is the Israel-Jordan peace treaty. Both parties recognized that arms control negotiations are a regional concern. They included a paragraph stating, "That the Parties undertake to work as a matter of priority, and as soon as possible, in the context of the Multilateral Working Group on Arms Control and Regional Security, and jointly, towards the creation of a Middle East free from weapons of mass destruction, both conventional, and non-conventional, in the context of a comprehensive, lasting and stable peace, characterized by the renunciation of the use of force, and by reconciliation, and goodwill."

Arms control in the Middle East will require regional and global cooperation. President George Bush articulated this point in 1991 when he stated the U.S. arms control objectives in the region: "Halting the proliferation of conventional and unconventional weapons in the Middle East, while supporting the legitimate need for every state to defend itself, will require the cooperation of many states in the region and around the world.[15]

As outlined in chapter 1 of this study, the multilateral ACRS working group has concentrated mainly on developing operational arms control measures: political-military and technical-military CSBMs. The process has also addressed some conceptual arms control topics such as threat perceptions, verification and monitoring, definition of the region for the purposes of arms control, and a future workshop on military doctrines. The ACRS process has not initiated discussions, however, on structural arms control of conventional and unconventional military holdings and capabilities.

Arab states argue that if structural arms control is not introduced then no meaningful progress in the ACRS process can take place. Even though the gradual implementation of political CSBMs could reduce the threat that a state perceives, military holdings and capabilities are still perceived

[15]Ann Devroy, "President Proposes Mideast Arms Curb; Suppliers Would Be Urged to Limit Sales," *Washington Post,* May 30, 1991, p. A1.

as the immediate threat. Typical factors that could be interpreted as military threats are strategic and tactical weapons holdings, weapon system characteristics, combined arms operations capability, geographic deployment of forces, ability to launch a surprise attack, and the military-industrial infrastructure that can provide the support required.

Responses by some regional states to such strategic threat perceptions have led to the introduction of weapons of mass destruction and their delivery systems into the region. These weapons have since had a decisive impact on the political-military dynamics of the region and on military operations.

Arab participants in the ACRS process argue that parallel to the development and implementation of a set of acceptable CSBMs, concepts of structural arms control should be introduced. This approach would form an initial arms control package. As the ACRS process evolves with progress in the bilateral peace negotiations, more ambitious CSBMs and some initial structural arms control measures could be implemented. These two measures, CSBMs and structural arms control, when integrated in the ACRS process, could be mutually reinforcing.

Producing an itemized ACRS agenda from the multilateral working group's "Statement on Arms Control and Regional Security," could be one approach to introducing structural arms control into the process. This could be done by first forming a group of technical experts to identify the elements required to address each issue. The next step would be to develop the modalities required to achieve the objectives outlined in the statement on an agreed schedule. In this approach all the items in the statement could be addressed concurrently, which would avoid arguments regarding the order and priority of the issues.

Regional Arab participants believe that the ACRS process and the new security environment have given the region an opportunity to start addressing control of unconventional and conventional weapons. The regional Arab countries maintain that the states attending the ACRS multilateral Middle East peace negotiations can be considered as an initial core of countries that have developed a set of arms control measures that are relevant in type and scope to the security requirements of the region. To eventually implement arms control measures fully, Iran, Iraq, and Syria should be fully integrated into the negotiation process.

Israel has repeatedly stated, however, that no structural arms control measures can be negotiated or implemented in the ACRS process as long as Iran, Iraq, and Syria remain outside the process. Israel points to Iran, in particular, as its biggest threat, with its potential of developing nuclear weapons and its long-range ballistic missiles that could strike Israel. Israel refuses to address the nuclear issue as long as Iran is not in the process.

With regard to international agreements such as the Non-Proliferation Treaty (NPT), the Chemical Weapons Convention (CWC), and the Biological Weapons Convention (BWC), the Arab states view them as a cornerstone of nonproliferation and as a first step toward eliminating weapons of mass destruction from the region. A means to an end and not an end by themselves, they are part of a bigger package that also contains security assurances in the form of declaratory statements, CSBMs, conflict prevention measures, conventional arms control measures, and the elimination of surface-to-surface missiles that could deliver weapons of mass destruction.

Within this comprehensive framework, Arab states believe that a weapons-of-mass-destruction–free zone (WMDFZ) could be defined as comprising the Arab League states, Israel, and Iran. These countries should then sign the NPT and all other global arms control agreements pertaining to weapons of mass destruction. With respect to verification, Arab states propose a combination of international and regional verification systems that complement each other. The Arab participants in the ACRS process have proposed studying the treaties of Tlatelolco and Rarotonga that created NWFZs in Latin America and in the South Pacific. The verification provisions of these models could complement international safeguards.

The Israeli approach is diametrically opposite. Israel maintains that a clear distinction should be made between an NWFZ and adherence to the NPT. In fact, Israel's declared policy is to negotiate an NWFZ with a regional verification and monitoring system in place, and then, when all this is achieved, it will sign the NPT.

Russia and the United States have recently agreed to pursue two new international treaties that would slow the proliferation of nuclear weapons. One such treaty is the "Fissile Material Cutoff," whose objective would be to stop the production of fissile material such as plutonium and enriched uranium. If Israel signs the treaty, it would have to shut down the Dimona nuclear weapons production facility and open all its nuclear reactors to international supervision. The treaty does not call for monitoring existing stockpiles; thus, countries would be permitted to retain current stockpiles without risking international intervention.

The other treaty, the Comprehensive Test Ban Treaty (CTBT), would ban testing of nuclear weapons, which would make it almost impossible for a proliferator to produce complex, multistage nuclear weapons or smaller and lighter nuclear weapons. Many in the Arab world believe that these treaties will fall short of eliminating nuclear weapons in the Middle East because they only curb the further production of new nuclear weapons but do not eliminate stockpiles.

Besides the Fissile Material Cutoff and the CTBT, positive security and negative security assurances and no-first-use declarations have been introduced to strengthen the resolve of countries to prevent the further spread of weapons of mass destruction. Positive security assurances are pledges to come to the assistance of a nonnuclear weapon state that is threatened. Negative security, on the other hand, is a pledge by nuclear weapons states not to use those weapons to threaten or attack a nonnuclear weapon state.

To many Arab states, "no-first-use" or "last resort" declarations by a nuclear weapon state can never be considered completely binding in case of war. These two declarations by themselves could be interpreted to imply the legitimization of nuclear weapons for military use in conventional conflicts, which would lead to an open-ended prescription for nuclear proliferation.

In conclusion, the Arab states' approach to ACRS entails taking steps to make the Middle East a zone free of weapons of mass destruction and their delivery systems; to prevent an arms race, particularly in advanced military technology; to prevent the military uses of outer space; to achieve greater transparency by the adoption of CSBMs; and to reduce conventional armed forces. The establishment of a weapons-of-mass-destruction–free zone in the region should be dealt with first in any arms control negotiations because such weapons increase threat perceptions exponentially.

The Future of Arab Security Policy

Given that a comprehensive peace has been achieved between Israel and the bordering Arab countries, it would be expected that the future regional security environment will require major changes in security policies and military strategies.

The future security policy of the Arab states will first and foremost be affected by the outcome of the PLO-Israel final status negotiations and the cooperative security nature of the Arab-Israeli comprehensive peace, whether it is "armed peace" or peace based on "cooperative security." It will also reflect future Israeli policy with respect to the NPT, its qualitative technological edge and military superiority, its offensive military doctrine, and its strategic military capabilities. Other regional factors will include: the proliferation of weapons of mass destruction and long-range ballistic missiles, the ACRS negotiations, the future of Iraq and its role in the region, and the perception of Iran as a threat to the Gulf region or as a partner in future security arrangements.

In light of this catalogue of factors affecting future security policy, political and economic support for the peace process by regional and extraregional countries is imperative. Peace in the Middle East will have a global impact. Regional instability will continue to threaten Gulf oil and hinder an overall Middle East peace settlement.

The Arab states will monitor the Israeli-Palestinian relationship for they expect that the outcome of the final status negotiations will be a State of Palestine in the West Bank and Gaza with East Jerusalem as its capital. The Arab world will be carefully scrutinizing Israel to make sure that, whatever party is in power, all agreements with the Palestinians are honored and the Palestinians feel confident that they will not be arbitrarily reoccupied by Israel. Given the history of the Arab-Israeli conflict, it will take some time to dispel fears and suspicions in Arab communities.

There will still be concern in the Arab world about Jewish extremists who want to stop peace talks between Israel and the Palestinians. Many Arab observers have expressed concern about the climate of violence created by the right-wing Israeli parties that led Baruch Goldstein to shoot and kill single-handedly twenty-nine Arabs while they were praying in a mosque, and Yig'al Amir to assassinate Yitzhak Rabin. Extremists full of hatred, hostility, and racial arrogance toward Arabs will be the main threat and source of tensions that could undermine peace. Many see these extremists using their guns to dictate their will to the Israeli government, even assassinating leaders to prevent giving back Palestinian land. If these extremists continue unchecked, they could easily trigger a reaction from the Palestinians that could bring the region back to political turmoil.

For the Arab states, arms control and nonproliferation of weapons of mass destruction will be at the heart of any future strategic security environment. Arab states will insist that Israel join the NPT. They will also be willing to accept the formation of a regional verification system that will complement international verification arrangements and ensure that all countries within the region adhere to the NPT, CWC, and the upcoming BWC.

Arab states will most probably seek to negotiate a reduction in Israel's strategic deterrence capability and a change in its offensive military doctrine. Arab states are convinced that reliance on military superiority alone cannot provide long-term security, and that real security is only achieved through political and military agreements. Arab analysts have expressed concern that Israel has not renounced the "weapons of last resort" doctrine. To many, Israel now has unquestioned superiority in conventional forces, faces no threat to its survival and basic security, and therefore has no need for nuclear weapons of last resort to defend itself. Arab states thus feel that Israel owes an answer to the question: Last resort against whom?

Continuing Security Threats

What remains threatening to Arab security is the Israeli nuclear capability: long-range delivery systems, such as the Jericho-IIB surface-to-surface missile, and long-range strike aircraft such as the F-15E/I. These aircraft are reported to have a 1,000-mile range that will enable the Israeli air force to strike deep into the countries of the Middle East, including Iran. The fear is that Israel could violate the airspace of adjacent Arab countries when launching a strike against a peripheral country and thereby drag the neighbor into a conflict. On the other hand, ballistic missiles carrying weapons of mass destruction launched at Israel could veer off course, land in Jordanian, Syrian, or Palestinian territory, and inflict catastrophic damage.

Arab observers find it unfortunate that some U.S. policymakers contend that Israel must be compensated with advanced military equipment for expected "territorial losses and increased security risks," in order to maintain its qualitative edge over the Arab states. A person unfamiliar with the conflict would get the impression that it was Israeli territory to start with, and Israel is giving it up rather than giving it back in return for peace. Second, it would seem that the Arab states adjacent to Israel would be the ones to breach the peace and are the only ones arming themselves for another possible confrontation with Israel. To many in the Arab world, this policy is biased toward Israel and completely disregards the risks and security concerns of the Arab states concluding peace treaties with Israel. This policy only heightens suspicions and tensions, which could result in an arms race in the region.

An important facet in the peace talks is the credibility of the Arab parties when they sign a peace treaty. It would seem that it is only the Arab countries that have to be checked to see if they keep their word. There has been a lot of talk about Syria and whether it will abide by a peace treaty with Israel. It is worth noting at this point that even during the 1982 war when Israeli and Syrian military forces were engaged in Lebanon, no incidents took place on the ground in the Golan Heights that either side would justify as a reason to start hostilities. In fact, Syria has kept to the letter of the 1974 cease-fire agreement with Israel.

Deterrence and Reassurance

As the Arab states and Israel conclude their peace agreements and work toward enhancing the security of the region, each could strike a balance between reassurance and deterrence: reassurance to strengthen the peace accords and deterrence to protect the peace from any external threats. The Arab states' concept of deterrence is one that is based on a qualitative conventional capability for self-defense that ensures self-reliance rather than one that relies on nuclear weapons and an offensive military force.

Strategies of reassurance consist basically of political-military CSBMs that are in the form of declarations of intent and can continue to be explored as new political and strategic developments take place. For example, each side could declare that it will refrain from the threat or use of force—conventional and unconventional—against the other, or of activities that threaten the security of the other.

When moving from bilateral security arrangements to regional security arrangements, one could proceed in two steps. The first step would be an outline of possible operational security arrangements that could be adopted by the Arab countries currently engaged in bilateral negotiations with Israel. In this initial stage, these Arab states would maintain stability and tranquillity along their borders with Israel by establishing mutually agreed upon demilitarized zones, air or land early warning systems, and joint border patrols.

These security arrangements are different from CSBMs that will have to be implemented on a bilateral basis in areas around the borders and between military forces. Once air, land, and sea CSBMs are implemented bilaterally, they could be complemented by CSBMs agreed to in the ACRS multilateral forum. These combined measures could then reinforce the bi-lateral security arrangements.

The next step would be to expand the circle to include Arab countries that are not directly involved but whose security is affected by the nature of the peace agreement. Multilateral arms control measures could then be introduced, and in this manner the bilateral and multilateral CSBMs will reinforce the bilateral security arrangements. Finally, countries that are pe-ripheral to the region but have political intentions and military capabilities that affect the region should be brought into the process. Iran, for exam-ple, would be informed of any regional security arrangements to ensure freedom of navigation in the Persian Gulf.

Arab states adjacent to Israel will probably not want Israel to play any military role in protecting their eastern borders. Each Arab country will insist on a military force for self-defense, and each will want self-reliance rather than outside assistance. Some Arab states, like Jordan and the GCC member states, lack sufficient manpower to defend their territories. They will compensate by investing in advanced technology weapon systems, es-pecially in air power and ground-based air defense systems to deter adver-saries, and by agreements with Western alliances.

Some analysts have envisioned regional security agreements based on the Damascus Declaration. Even though the Damascus Declaration was not implemented, it dealt with Gulf security, and it seems to have set the conceptual foundation for a possible Arab "collective security" arrange-ment that would only address military threats. This could consist of the GCC plus a number of Arab countries, while another configuration could include Israel. The GCC member states, however, will most probably find it politically difficult to have a large number of foreign troops in their territories, even if they are Arab troops and especially if they are from Israel. Some Arab and Western analysts maintain that for the GCC coun-tries, Israel could not be considered a major player in maintaining stability in the Gulf region.

For the near future, however, the GCC countries will continue building their defense forces up to a level that will make any direct confrontation as costly as possible to any adversaries. In any high-intensity conflict with Iran or Iraq, they are well aware that individually and collectively they will not be able to match the size of the military forces of their adversaries. As such, in any military crisis the GCC countries' fundamental strategy against military aggression will be to provide the initial deterrent forces in the form of advanced technology weapon systems and agreements with Western alliances. If this deterrent fails, the armed forces of the GCC member states will be expected to delay the opposing forces until such time as international over-the-horizon reinforcements in manpower and military equipment from the Western allies arrive.

Some Arab analysts expect that in the post-Saddam era, Iraq will play a pivotal role in the Arab-Israeli and Gulf regions. Iraq's vast oil resources, population, and strategic depth (looked at from within the region and from its geographic location as a frontier state) make it an essential participant in any regional security arrangements.

Conclusion

The conflicts in the region have fundamentally altered the economic structure of the region. States have been dissipating their national resources to buy weapons and build arms industries, thereby neglecting other sectors of their economies. The Arab states realize that curbing proliferation and preventing conflicts would enable them to devote greater attention to the economic and social problems of the region.

Due to the complexity of the possible sources of conflict, the growing number of participants within the region, the economic and political interdependence of the countries within the region, and the involvement of peripheral and outside countries, a Middle East security and cooperation forum has been proposed to address a wide range of military and nonmilitary security-related issues. The nonmilitary security-related issues could include socioeconomic development, energy, water, the environment, population, and human rights. One such forum was proposed by Jordan in 1991, a Conference on Security and Cooperation in the Middle East (CSCME). The goals of our proposed Middle East Cooperative Security Framework (see p. 89 in chapter 4) are basically similar to those of the CSCME.

If all means at the disposal of the regional security arrangements fail to maintain international peace, then the region could fall back on some regional collective security system. Clearly, a fully developed cooperative security framework would include a proviso for collective action as a guarantee to its participants. Cooperative security and collective security could be mutually reinforcing. In other words, security defined as the absence of the threat of war is dependent on both political and military stability. Military and political stability complement each other, and security will be enhanced if political and military stability are high. The requirement in the peace-building phase will be a regional cooperative security relationship that is comprehensive. Military and nonmilitary resources can be integrated to respond to threats and to deal with aggression. In this way, the framework will be able to maintain peace and stability in the region.

4

Bridging the Gap: Resolving the Security Dilemma in the Middle East

Shai Feldman and Abdullah Toukan

FOR ALMOST FIVE DECADES, states in the Middle East have made every attempt to enhance their security, mostly with little regard to the extent to which these efforts have undermined the security of their neighbors. This was unfortunate because while short-term security requirements could be met in such a fashion, in the longer term this policy proved self-defeating. States whose security was negatively affected by their neighbors' security-enhancing measures took steps to diminish the perceived threat. In turn, these countermeasures sometimes reduced the security of the state whose security-enhancing efforts began the chain reaction. This points to the main dilemma of international and regional security: how states might enhance their security without thereby diminishing the security of their neighbors. Addressing this dilemma and suggesting methods of mitigating its effects in the Middle East is the main purpose of this chapter.

As the second and third chapters of this book demonstrate, the considerable progress made in Arab–Israeli peacemaking in recent years has not removed all concerns of the region's states with regard to one another's political intentions, military and strategic capabilities, and defense doctrines. While a serious attempt to begin addressing these concerns was launched in early 1992 in the framework of the Arms Control and Regional Security (ACRS) working group, a significant number of Middle East states remain outside the process. Moreover, even among the parties taking part in the ACRS talks, the progress made is yet to result in a meaningful consensus regarding the nature and true magnitude of their remaining concerns as well as about the best manner of addressing them.

The first sections of this chapter elaborate the gap that still needs to be bridged between the parties' security concerns and their views with regard to the best manner of addressing them. Then, proposals for closing this gap and enhancing Middle East regional security will be made at five levels: (1) affecting the manner in which the region's states think about their security affairs; (2) strengthening the process launched by the ACRS working group of the multilateral Middle East peace negotiations; (3) expanding the Middle East track-II talks; (4) establishing a Middle East Cooperative Security Framework (MECSF) to enhance the security of the region's states through military as well as nonmilitary means; and (5) ensuring America's continued engagement in the Middle East.

Arab Concerns

The breakthroughs achieved in Arab–Israeli peacemaking in recent years did not eliminate all sources of Arab concern with regard to Israel's strategic capabilities and its military force structure and doctrine. Primarily, Arab states continue to express their uneasiness with regard to Israel's nuclear potential and its implications for regional stability. Their assessment is that Israel already enjoys an unquestioned conventional superiority and that in the new regional security environment emerging in the aftermath of the peace agreements between Israel and the adjacent Arab countries and the PLO, Israel no longer faces military threats to its existence that might justify the possession of nuclear weapons as a strategic deterrent or as a "weapon of last resort."

At the conceptual level, Arabs view the nuclear issue as representing a core issue of the Arab–Israeli conflict. In their eyes, Israel's acquisition of strategic and conventional deterrence, coupled with its offensive military posture, produced a provocative political atmosphere rather than an environment conducive to the prevention of conflict and war. The Arab states also believe that Israel's alleged nuclear doctrine of "weapon of last resort" would not be binding in case of war. In their view it should be interpreted instead as implying the legitimization of nuclear weapons for military purposes in conventional confrontations, and therefore as an open-ended prescription for nuclear proliferation.

Consequently, the Arab states demand that Israel sign the 1968 nuclear Non-Proliferation Treaty (NPT) and open its nuclear facilities to international inspections. Arab states insist that international instruments such as the NPT enhance national security. They view the NPT as a stand-alone international legal instrument that should not be made hostage to regional politics. In this context Arab states insist that the first stage of implementing nuclear arms control in the region would be universal membership in the NPT and international monitoring of all nuclear facilities. They also regard the support of such international instruments as consistent with the idea that the substance and aims of the regional arms control and security-building process should complement the substance and pace of international global arms control instruments. These Arab states do not exclude the possibility that the second stage of implementing arms control agreements will focus on regional frameworks.

The Arab states also do not consider Iran to be a threat to Israel's existence. Consequently, they reject suggestions that the signing of global arms control agreements should be made contingent on Iran's behavior. Moreover, in their judgment peace agreements between Israel and Egypt, Jordan, Lebanon, Syria, and the Palestinians would deprive Iran of any political context in which to confront Israel.

Arab states also believe that an Israeli decision to join the NPT will provide the ACRS process a much-needed boost. Such a step is viewed as potentially making it easier for Arab states to begin considering and implementing more ambitious confidence- and security-building measures (CSBMs) and structural arms control in the conventional realm.

Yet the nuclear issue is not the only component of Israeli deterrence that Arab states continue to find troubling. As mentioned earlier, these states regard Israel's offensive military doctrine, the high mobility of the IDF's force structure allowing the implementation of this doctrine, and Israel's commitment to maintaining the qualitative edge of its armed forces as threatening regional stability and their national security. In this context even Arab analysts who view Israel's motivation for adopting this doctrine and force structure as defensive emphasize that Arab states cannot ignore the possibility that this capability will be used by a future Israeli government for offensive purposes.

The Arab states also reject Israel's insistence that it must possess the capacity to deter and defend against a potential coalition of Arab armed forces. They view the peace process as ending the Arab–Israeli conflict, and they regard force and contingency planning against a reemergence of an Arab war coalition as inconsistent with Mideast peace. They also see Israel's desire to balance such a coalition as leading to a continuing arms race and a way of establishing and maintaining Israeli military dominance in the region—a proposition they find unacceptable.

At the political–strategic level, Arabs fear that the peace process may be stalled or reversed by political change in Israel. The new Israeli government might avoid meaningful Israeli–Palestinian final status negotiations and prevent Israeli–Syrian and Israeli–Lebanese accords by rejecting the return of territories and a withdrawal of IDF forces. It is feared that such a development would rekindle Arab–Israeli violence in the West Bank and across adjacent Arab states and result eventually in another Arab–Israeli war. Such a war might be extremely devastating, possibly escalating to the use of mass destruction weapons.

Israeli Concerns

On its part, Israel remains uncertain about the future of its regional security environment. It views the Middle East as an arena that continues to experience a grand struggle between the forces of the old and the new Middle East—those supporting Arab–Israeli accommodation and regional economic development and those opposed to the Madrid peace process and determined to erode economic development with the hope that the resulting public resentment might hasten revolutionary change. Within this context Israel is particularly concerned about the numerous Iranian public statements reflecting deep hostility toward Israel as well as by Iran's perceived attempts to acquire a nuclear potential and ballistic missiles that could reach Israel.

At the same time, Israelis are concerned that support for peacemaking is thin even among Arab countries that concluded peace agreements with Israel, and they are worried that these Arab governments face considerable domestic opposition. In turn, this breeds an Israeli fear that a possible triumph of Arab forces who are opposed to the peace process might result in its reversal. In this context Israelis continue to feel uneasy about the many strengths of the Arab states—their vast territories, large populations, oil resources and resulting wealth, and their ability to field large, regular conventional forces.

Moreover, Israel's view is that in the aftermath of the bilateral peace agreements, Arab countries no longer face serious military threats. In this new security environment, Israel sees little reason for Egypt, Syria, and other Arab states to continue maintaining large conventional force structures. The fact that, despite the absence of serious external threats, Egypt invests enormous resources in modernizing its large armed forces continues to puzzle many Israelis.

While the peace agreements to be concluded between Israel and Syria and Israel and Lebanon hold the promise of completing the bilateral peace process between Israel and all its immediate Arab neighbors—thus improving the chances of Israel's complete integration in the region—the depth of territorial withdrawals that Israel is required to make is widely viewed as only increasing its strategic vulnerability. In the judgment of some Israelis, this should lead their country to maintain its qualitative edge as well as other components of its grand strategy—such as its offensive military doctrine—as a hedge against a possible reversal of the Arab–Israeli peace process.

In Israel's view, a similar logic applies to its nuclear policy. While Israel shares the nuclear nonproliferation objectives reflected in the NPT, it regards the signing of the treaty and the transparency entailed in exposing its nuclear facilities to full-scope safeguards as inconsistent with the imperative of maintaining its ambiguous nuclear status. This ambiguity has been part of Israel's national security concept for a number of decades. In Israel's view this posture should not be altered until all serious threats to its security and survival have been removed.

In this context, Israel places continued emphasis on the hostile intentions and growing capabilities of Iran, particularly its interest in developing a nuclear option. Israel is determined to deter such threats and would not accept a major erosion of its deterrence until this threat is removed. This also explains Israel's approach to the region's delineation: since Iran presents a major potential threat, structural arms control cannot be applied in the Middle East until Iran is incorporated into the new regime and assumes all the constraints and limitations entailed in its establishment.

Finally, Israel's judgment is that once conditions are ripe for structural arms control in the nuclear realm, a regionally focused agreement would be far more effective than existing international instruments. In Israel's view, such an approach, reflected in the suggested weapons-of-mass-destruction–free zone, would provide a much closer match between arms control and the efforts to advance conflict resolution and confidence building in the region. In addition, as the Tlatelolco treaty transforming Latin America into a nuclear weapon–free zone (NWFZ) demonstrates, such an approach would allow the adoption of far more effective verification measures than those currently associated with the NPT: in addition to IAEA full-scope safeguards, such an agreement would allow the construction of a regional verification mechanism and the adoption of reciprocal on-site inspections.

Bridging the Gap

As the preceding sections illustrate, there remains a wide gap between the threat perceptions and security concerns of Israel and the Arab states as well as in their continued tendency to exacerbate the security dilemma by attempting to increase their security at the expense of their neighbors. In the next sections we propose five mutually reinforcing avenues for bridging the gap between the parties' perceptions and concerns and for helping them resolve the security dilemma or at least mitigate its effects.

Changing Security Perceptions

The prerequisite for building institutions and mechanisms allowing the region's states to mitigate the security dilemma is that they begin to think differently about their national security affairs. In the first instance, governments must become aware of the security dilemma. Awareness of the dilemma is essential for persuading states that when alternative modes for enhancing security exist, efforts should be made to pursue those that promise a substantial measure of security while posing the least threat to neighboring states. Governments might then forgo steps that may result in improved short-term security if they become aware that such steps would result in diminished security in the long term. Overall, this implies that governments cease thinking about maximizing security at all costs and begin to think about striking a new balance between deterrence and reassurance, between meeting their security requirements and attending to the security perceptions of their neighbors.

A related required perceptual change is that states begin to view arms control and confidence building as part of their national security policy. Embedded in their previously hostile environment is the tendency of most states in the Middle East to regard any limitation on their freedom of action, such as the imposition of transparency measures, as potentially detrimental to their national security. With a less-hostile environment emerging, the region's states must begin to realize that constraints on their freedom of action may result in enhanced security if these limitations reduce their neighbors' anxieties and propensity to take dangerous action.

Finally, as the Middle East is slowly transformed into a more benign environment, the region's states must drop another mode of thinking characteristic of hostile relationships: the tendency to exaggerate threats and to emphasize their own vulnerabilities and weaknesses. For example, greater familiarity with Israeli society may persuade Arabs that they can safely abandon fears that their states, with a combined population of some 250 million, could suffer from the "hegemonic designs" of a country with a population of about 5 million. Similarly, Israelis might remember that their "soft belly" is less soft than is commonly believed: the IDF does not face a serious challenger along Israel's eastern border and would have ample time to react if such a challenge were to result from the entry of any large expeditionary forces into Jordan.

A more balanced assessment of their security problems based on a less exaggerated view of their neighbors' capabilities and intentions and a more accurate appreciation of their own strengths would lead Middle East states to diminish their propensity to take measures that exacerbate the security dilemma. Thus, the tendency to take unilateral self-help measures would be gradually replaced by an emerging "common security culture," focused on enhancing overall security in the region. Clearly, it would be unrealistic to expect the region's states to complete such a dramatic mental transformation prior to the achievement of comprehensive peace. Their governments and influential elites, however, should be encouraged to begin thinking differently about their countries' security without delay.

Enhancing the ACRS Process

The second important step that can be taken to strengthen security in the Middle East is to enhance the ACRS talks. These discussions, sponsored by Russia and the United States, are conducted as one of the five working groups launched by the organizational meeting of the multilateral Middle East peace negotiations in Moscow in early 1992. At the outset of the ACRS talks, the Arab states and Israel disagreed about the agenda. The Arab states stressed that these talks should first deal with the danger of nuclear proliferation in the region, since this involves the most destructive and hence the most destabilizing weapons. Conversely, Israel argued that sensitive issues involving the parties' strategic deterrence can be dealt with only after a high level of mutual confidence and trust has been established. As a compromise, the regional participants agreed that structural arms control should be addressed parallel to a Helsinki-type and Stockholm-type confidence- and security-building process and await progress in the bilateral Arab–Israeli negotiations.

In this spirit the parties accepted the cosponsors' suggestion that the ACRS talks address two main issues: the definition of "visionary goals" for arms control in the Middle East—in this framework the nuclear issue could achieve its due prominence—and a parallel effort to implement confidence- and security-building measures. To carry out this agenda, external sponsors were nominated to orchestrate the work on each of the main items: Russia and the United States for the effort to define the objectives of arms control in the Middle East; Canada for confidence building in the maritime realm; Turkey for the exchange of military information and prenotification of major military movements; and the Netherlands for communication.

Three factors contributed to the success of the ACRS talks. First, little media attention was given to their proceedings, which made them less exposed to political sensitivities. Second, the intersessional meetings conducted in their framework, free of media attention, provided an excellent setting for informal discussions and greater familiarity between senior officers of the region's armed forces. There were numerous frank exchanges allowing better understanding of each other's requirements and concerns. Finally, the cosponsors of this process exercised the right balance between guidance and nonintervention. While providing essential assistance, they avoided any attempt to impose themselves, particularly in determining the outcome of these talks.

By late 1993 the work of the various intersessional meetings was reorganized in the form of two "baskets": the conceptual basket was primarily intended to define the ultimate objectives of confidence building and arms control in the region and to produce a political-declaratory confidence-building and arms control measure by formulating and making public a "Statement on Arms Control and Regional Security" defining these objectives. In parallel the operational basket was intended to advance the wide array of technical–military CSBMs described earlier.

From 1992 to 1994 impressive progress was made in negotiating CSBMs in the framework of the ACRS talks. A regional communication system was initiated, at first serving the exchange of information related to ACRS activities. It was temporarily attached to the CSCE Communication Center in the Netherlands but is intended to be permanently located in Cairo within the next few years. Also, the parties decided to establish a Regional Security Center (RSC) in Jordan with related facilities in Qatar and Tunisia. In addition to performing similar functions to the CSCE Conflict Prevention Center (CPC) in Vienna, the proposed regional body would study and carry out more long-term conflict resolution activities. The RSC would also provide training in conflict prevention, conflict management and resolution, and confidence building and arms control for young interns from governments and NGOs throughout the Middle East.

The ACRS talks also made considerable progress in advancing specific confidence-building measures. By early 1995 understandings were reached on two maritime security-building measures: cooperation in search-and-rescue (SAR) operations and in preventing incidents at sea (IAS). Another consensus was obtained regarding prenotification of major military activities, exercises and other movement of forces, and on a more general exchange of military-related data.

Yet in all cases it was agreed that participation in the mechanisms adopted and the activities proposed would take place on a voluntary and reciprocal basis. Indeed, the parties have not yet agreed to implement a set of confidence- and security-building measures on a regionwide basis. This suggests that some parties were still unsure about the implications of the ACRS process and its future, and that the region was still in transition to a new security environment.

At the same time, an objective examination of the ACRS talks must yield the conclusion that they have been an impressive success. The starting point of these talks was much more complex than that of the NATO–

Warsaw Pact talks of the mid-1970s: As a multilateral process the ACRS discussions were bound to be more complicated than the bilateral East–West process. Also, the Middle East talks were initiated between parties that had a recent history of bloody battles, whereas the European process was free of the emotional heritage of violence. NATO and Warsaw Pact forces never fought one another.

Moreover, by the time the Helsinki Final Act was concluded, it had been some thirty years since the parties involved were last engaged in a deadly conflict. In contrast to the near-total absence of direct discourse between the Arab states and Israel until President Sadat's journey to Jerusalem in late 1977, the Soviet Union and the United States maintained an embassy in each other's capital and kept open channels of communication between their respective governments throughout the Cold War. Still, it took the two blocs some ten years to travel from Helsinki to the Stockholm agreement. By contrast, in less than four years the ACRS talks yielded a draft document at least as ambitious as the Helsinki Final Act and a series of CSBMs, some of which extend beyond those adopted at Stockholm.

Its enormous success notwithstanding, the ACRS process has already reached a crossroads at which the parties must choose a future course: the place of nuclear arms control on the ACRS agenda. The process may encounter two other crossroads as well: the possible entrance of Syria and Lebanon into the talks, and engaging other members of the Arab League and Iran.

Nuclear Arms Control

So far, the ACRS discussions have yielded an embryonic regional CSBM regime and a document charting the ultimate purposes of the process—agreed upon by the parties involved except for one item: the parties' commitments in the realm of nuclear arms control. This progress has been consistent with the sequential approach adopted in the East-West context. The CSBM regime inaugurated in Helsinki and Stockholm created the conditions allowing the negotiation of structural arms control agreements: the Intermediate-range Nuclear Forces (INF) in Europe, the Strategic Arms Reduction Treaty (START), and the Conventional Armed Forces in Europe (CFE) treaty.

However, while this sequence met Israel's priorities as well as its objective of gaining Arab recognition and increased integration in the region, it did not accord with the urgency with which Arab states regard the task of negotiating structural arms control, particularly in the nuclear realm. By mid-1995 there was a danger that the disappointment of Arab states at their failure to obtain Israeli signature of the NPT during the April Review and Extension Conference would also have a negative impact on the ACRS process.

On the other hand, there are at least two significant reasons why the transition to structural arms control is bound to be more difficult and hence must be managed more carefully in the Middle East than it was in the East-West negotiations. Most important, there are different structural asymmetries in the region. Some were purposefully developed in order to compensate for the others: the development of Israel's nuclear option was seen as part of its response to the Arab states' numerical advantage, while the acquisition of surface-to-surface missiles by a number of Arab states was viewed as compensating for the qualitative superiority of the Israeli air force. These historical and substantive linkages reveal the difficulty of negotiating one structural asymmetry without simultaneously addressing others as well.

Second, in East–West (NATO–Warsaw Pact and Soviet–U.S.) negotiations, all relevant parties were present. Thus, in the framework of the INF and CFE treaties, all countries possessing relevant capabilities were involved, and START negotiations avoided lower ceilings that might have required taking the nuclear forces of other parties—Britain, China, and France—into account. By contrast, key Middle East players remain outside the ACRS process: Lebanon and Syria have so far declined invitations to join the talks, while other members of the Arab League and Iran remain outside the process. Given that most of these states possess relevant force structures and are major sources of proliferation concerns, it is difficult to see how negotiations on structural arms control in the Middle East could be conducted without their participation.

While these problems present significant obstacles to structural arms control negotiations, Arab concerns could be taken into consideration by initiating a preparatory process in which the parties could enter extensive but informal preliminary consultations on the requirements of structural arms control in the region: identifying the relevant participants, examining the preconditions for negotiations and implementation, ascertaining the linkages between the various issues and the best ways of managing these linkages, and studying alternative methods of verifying compliance with prospective agreements. In addition to track-I talks (formal negotiations between governments), the parties may adopt a track-II approach, allowing consultations and the commissioning of studies by international experts on the issues involved. Use could also be made of the proposed RSC in Jordan and the related facilities in Qatar and Tunisia for conducting some of the requisite studies.

While beginning to meet Arab priorities, Israel's concerns would have to be addressed about the possibility that the ACRS talks might slide prematurely into negotiating structural arms control that focuses exclusively on the nuclear issue. For this purpose, a clear understanding would have to be reached that structural arms control must involve all major categories of weapons: conventional weapons, ballistic missiles, and chemical, biological, and nuclear arms. This will allow the launching of initial discussions on conventional force reductions as well as on the possible transformation of the region into a zone free of all weapons of mass destruction.

Israel's concerns about the possibility that structural arms control discussions may experience a "slippery slope" slide into premature substantive negotiations might also be alleviated by a better appreciation of the obstacles facing any such discussions and, consequently, of the length of time it would take to resolve the problems entailed. Indeed, while in Europe it took over ten years from the initiation of the Mutual and Balanced Force Reduction (MBFR) talks to the conclusion of the CFE treaty, discussions of a similar nature in the Middle East are likely to take even longer. This can be expected in light of the many asymmetries that discussions of structural arms control in the Middle East would have to confront: the parties' very different threat perceptions and the fact that most of the region's states face threats of varying magnitude from several directions; the asymmetry in the quality and quantities of their armed forces and the different weapons systems deployed by these forces; their different sensitivity to casualties; their differing ability to bear financial and other costs; the disparity in geography and in the resulting distribution of tactical and strategic depth; the cultural-technological asymmetries and the resulting gaps in the pace of mobilization and in the rate at which new weapons systems can be absorbed and integrated into the existing force structures; and finally, differences in political systems and their effect on options for mass mobilization.

Peace between Israel, Syria, and Lebanon

A second crossroad that the ACRS talks might reach within the next years involves the possible peace agreements between Israel, Syria, and Lebanon. When this occurs, it would be important to make every effort to integrate Syria and Lebanon into the ACRS process. Both countries refused to join any of the multilateral talks until there is a breakthrough in their bilateral negotiations with Israel. Given the size and composition of Syria's armed forces and its strategic role in the region, Syria's participation would be essential both for a meaningful application of regionwide CSBMs and for conducting structural arms control consultations and eventual negotiations and implementation.

It should be noted that within the ACRS process, every effort was made to ensure that when additional parties joined the process, their constructive suggestions would be taken into account. Nevertheless, ACRS participants should reaffirm that matters concluded within the framework of their talks will not be reopened to objections aimed at jeopardizing the success of the process.

Other Members of the Arab League and Iran

A much more sensitive issue concerns the future relationship between the ACRS talks and relevant parties who have not been invited. Some of the members of the Arab League and Iran remain significant regional powers and comprise major sources of proliferation concern. As noted earlier, it would be impossible to implement comprehensive CSBMs as well as structural arms control in the Middle East without their active participation.

The integration of some of these parties into the ACRS process has become all the more important in light of the advent of modern technology. Until recently, security issues in the Arab–Israeli arena could be considered separately from Gulf security issues. The Gulf region was not directly affected by the 1948, 1956, 1967, 1970, and 1973 Arab–Israeli wars, and eight years of the Iran–Iraq war did not affect the Arab–Israeli arena. This is no longer the case. The proliferation of long-range ballistic missiles as well as long-range strike aircraft has made the two subregions sensitive to developments in one another. This was experienced clearly during the 1991 Gulf War when Iraq fired more than forty extended-range SCUD missiles at Israel. It illustrates most clearly that limitations on ballistic missiles in the Middle East cannot be applied in only one of the two subregions; rather they would have to be applied in the region at large.

In view of the bloody history of the Arab–Israeli conflict, the modest progress made in the framework of the ACRS talks should be considered quite remarkable. At the same time, it should be recognized that these talks have reached one important juncture that will determine their future vitality: the ability to weave preliminary consultations regarding the prospects of structural arms control into the process. Two other important junctures will be: the manner in which ACRS participants will deal with the possible entry of Lebanon and Syria into the ACRS talks, and the extent to which efforts should be made to engage other Arab League members and Iran in the ACRS talks.

Whether the ACRS framework can survive these challenges remains an open question, particularly given the interrelationships between some of the decisions entailed. For example, the implementation of comprehensive structural arms control is extremely unlikely without the participation of all major sources of proliferation concern. Yet the admission of these states into the process would require a major policy change on the part of all the parties concerned.

Future Phases of the ACRS Process

What, then, is the sequence of developments in the ACRS process that we envisage? How is it likely to be linked to the evolving bilateral efforts to resolve the Arab–Israeli conflict? At the present phase of the peace process—following the establishment of Egyptian–Israeli and Israeli–Jordanian peace, the implementation of the Declaration of Principles (DOP) between Israel and the Palestinians, and the intermittent Israeli–Syrian and Israeli–Lebanese negotiations—the parties should make the proposed Regional Security Center operational, using it as a principal venue for conducting seminars and training on concepts of arms control and regional security. In addition, preliminary discussions could be held regarding competing concepts of structural arms control and regional monitoring and verification techniques. This could lead to a consensus regarding the text of a "Statement on Arms Control and Regional Security" in the Middle East.

The second phase would be characterized by the signing of bilateral peace agreements between Israel and Syria and Israel and Lebanon and by meaningful progress in Israeli–Palestinian final status negotiations. At this stage the RSC would be functioning in Jordan as well as in Qatar and Tunisia, a regional communication system would be established in Cairo, and a set of CSBMs would be fully implemented by ACRS participants: prenotification of military exercises, exchange of military information, and joint exercises of mechanisms and procedures for avoiding incidents at sea and for cooperating in search-and-rescue operations. In addition, mechanisms required for structural arms control negotiations and for establishing appropriate verification and monitoring systems could be elaborated. Within this framework, consensus would be reached regarding the definition of the Middle East region, which would determine the countries participating in the envisaged negotiations.

The third phase would follow the conclusion of Israeli–Palestinian final status negotiations and the successful implementation of the agreement reached, as well as the participation of Iran and Iraq in the peace process and the fulfillment of other conditions allowing their inclusion in regional arms control negotiations. At this phase, implementation of structural arms control and associated verification and monitoring systems, as well as operational confidence- and security-building measures, would begin. In addition, the scope of RSC activities would be expanded to include crisis management, conflict resolution, and conflict prevention.

Expanding Track-II Talks

Regional and bilateral peace and security in the Middle East can also be enhanced by maintaining and expanding the channels for track-II discussions between the region's states. This refers to the parties' ability to engage each other in informal talks regarding their respective aspirations and objectives, their threat perceptions and security concerns, and the manner in which they propose to meet their objectives and to address their sources of concern. These track-II talks can be conducted in informal settings by independent scholars and senior journalists as well as by government officials and senior military officers acting in an independent capacity.

Track-II talks have already proven to be very useful in Arab–Israeli peacemaking. Lengthy informal discussions between independent Israeli scholars and PLO officials, held under the auspices of Norway's Institute for Applied Social Sciences (FAFO), paved the way to the September 1993 Israel–PLO Oslo agreement. As noted earlier, this agreement had enormous impact on other dimensions of Arab–Israeli negotiations, eventually leading to the Israel–Jordan peace treaty.

Less dramatic but equally significant, track-II discussions have also been useful in supporting the ACRS process and in advancing the dialogue on security and arms control in the Middle East. Some of these discussions took place during the late 1980s, but their intensity increased dramatically after the 1991 Gulf War. These talks were conducted under the auspices of a large number of research institutes and nongovernmental organizations: the Quakers, PUGWASH, the Search for Common Ground, the Carnegie Endowment for International Peace, the American Academy of Arts and Sciences, the Mershon Center at Ohio State University, the Institut Français des Rélations Internationales, the American Association for the Advancement of Science, the University of California's Institute on Global Conflict and Cooperation, and the University of California at Los Angeles.

These activities could not have taken place without the support provided by a number of philanthropic foundations, primarily Carnegie Corporation, the Ford Foundation, the Rockefeller Foundation, and the Ploughshares Fund. On some occasions government financial assistance was essential to the success of these nongovernment activities. Notably, the U.S. Department of Energy played an important role in allowing a number of track-II meetings to take place.

The most important advantage of these talks is that their informal character allows participants to explore sensitive issues that cannot be discussed in formal negotiations and to examine possibilities for resolving problems in an uncommitted fashion. Equally important, the informal settings and frameworks in which these discussions take place allow participants to express their perceptions and concerns and to learn about their neighbors' worries and fears. By sharing their experience and impressions with their countries' government officials, participants can improve the understanding of their governments' track-I negotiators.

Track-II talks may prove particularly useful in advancing the prospects for arms control and regional security in the Middle East when the ACRS track-I talks reach a deadlock. Under such circumstances, unofficial and nonbinding discussions can help the search for ways of overcoming the stalemate. When conditions hinder the parties' ability to overcome the deadlock, track-II talks can reduce tensions and mitigate other possible negative consequences of the stalemate. In addition, they allow partici-pants in track-I talks to stay in touch with one another, so that the gains made in the interpersonal dimensions of the ACRS talks are not lost.

Another important potential advantage of the track-II frameworks is that in principle they enable the participation of individuals from states that have opted to stay out of the ACRS talks or that have not been invited to take part in these deliberations. In the past this allowed a better appreci-ation of Syria's perceptions and concerns as well as a better understanding of Lebanon's fears and aspirations. In the future, changes in Iran and Iraq may allow more effective participation in track-II talks by individuals from Tehran and Baghdad. The key role of these countries that affect security in the Gulf states and in the Middle East at large makes their eventual partici-pation in these talks essential.

Given their proven utility and the low level of risk involved, every possi-ble effort must be made to maintain these channels of informal communi-cation and to expand their scope and intensity. This is important even when rapid progress is made in track-I discussions—notably the ACRS talks—because formal negotiations are bound to experience occasional dif-ficulties. Even if these formal negotiations are concluded successfully, the implementation of the resulting agreements is often associated with ten-sions that must be defused. Therefore, continuous track-II talks may be useful during formal negotiations as well as in their aftermath.

Constructing a Middle East Cooperative Security Framework

While the ACRS process has already achieved considerable success—in absolute terms and particularly by Middle East standards—one realm in which it has not had sufficient impact is in changing public perceptions. Only a small number of senior officials and nongovernment observers in the countries taking part in the ACRS talks are aware that a new, if still limited, spirit of cooperation is developing between Israel and a large num-ber of Arab states. Paradoxically, this lack of awareness is the result of a major source of the success of the ACRS process: the same low visibility that made the process less sensitive politically is also responsible for the fact that the publics of the region's states remain largely unaware of its achievements.

The danger entailed in this lack of awareness is that peoples' thinking would continue to be conditioned by the logic of "the old Middle East," which would make current positive developments too easy to reverse. To diminish this danger, the ACRS process should be complemented by the establishment of a Middle East Cooperative Security Framework (MECSF). The proposed MECSF would be based on Article VIII of the United Nations Charter calling for the creation of "regional arrangements or agencies for dealing with such matters relating to the maintenance of international peace and security as are appropriate for regional action, provided that such arrangements or agencies and their activities are consistent with the purposes of the U.N."

The purpose of the new framework would be to enhance the security of the region's states through military as well as nonmilitary means. In the foreseeable future the new framework would not replace the ACRS process nor would it replicate the measures already considered and the arrangements already adopted by ACRS participants. In this sense it would initially differ from the Conference on Security and Cooperation in Europe, in the framework of which many of the measures proposed at the ACRS talks were originally implemented in Europe.

The principal difference between the MECSF and the ACRS talks would be that the MECSF would be run by the region's states, not by external sponsors. Hence, the creation of the MECSF would itself signal to the various publics in the region that the Middle East peace process has matured. This message would be transmitted powerfully by the manner in which the MECSF is conducted. Its annual conference would be given high visibility and the parties' delegations would be chaired by their respective heads of state or their ministers of foreign affairs or defense.

This is not meant to exclude the participation of outside powers in the proposed MECSF. Quite the contrary, countries that affect the region's security and prosperity should be encouraged to join the MECSF as associate members. As elaborated below, this applies especially to the United States, whose unique role in maintaining and enhancing the region's stability makes its participation in the MECSF essential. Similarly, Russia's proximity to the region and its historical role and interests in the Middle East justify that it take an active part in all MECSF deliberations and activities.

Another major distinction between the two forums is that while the ACRS talks focus on arms control and confidence building, the MECSF would also deal with conflict prevention through the eventual integration of the RSC into its framework. As such, the MECSF would devote a large part of its energy and resources to mitigating the sources of conflict in the region and to addressing factors that sustain high levels of tension: from tangible border demarcation disputes to less tangible factors such as the propagation of myths and the propensity to portray adversaries in demonic terms. For this purpose, the MECSF would engage in different activities, ranging from preventive diplomacy—including the "standby" availability of multinational teams of diplomats ready to be dispatched to resolve disputes before they escalate into full-scale conflict—to programs designed to move the region from confrontational security policies into cooperative security frameworks.

In attempting to diminish the propensity for mythmaking and demonization in the region, the MECSF would conduct a significant regionwide educational effort to demolish the various myths held by different publics about one another. For example, it could dispel the myth held by many Israelis that "Jordan is Palestine," that the Hashemite Kingdom of Jordan could be transformed into an entity that would meet the Palestinians' demand for independent statehood. The myth held by many Arabs that they are threatened by Israel's determination to expand "from the Nile to the Euphrates" could be similarly debunked.

A major effort that the MECSF could undertake in this context is to help delete myths and expressions of demonization from textbooks used in schools throughout the region. This would require that committees nominated by the MECSF would examine these textbooks and that once myths and expressions of demonization are identified, they would recommend changes in the text. Related to this, the MECSF could convene meetings of historians from the region's various states and encourage them to bridge gaps between competing interpretations of their past relations. This might diminish the likelihood that disagreement about their histories would contribute in the future to the type of violence experienced in the Balkans.

The contrast between the proposed MECSF and the ACRS talks would also be manifested in other important respects. While ACRS and other working groups initiated by the 1992 Moscow conference were designed to support the Arab–Israeli bilateral peace process launched in Madrid, the MECSF is intended to strengthen security and cooperation in the region at large. As such, it would address issues that affect the region's security but are independent of Arab–Israeli peacemaking. In this sense the

MECSF would be a much more truly multilateral process than the Madrid framework.

In addition, while the ACRS talks have addressed the military dimensions of security almost exclusively, the MECSF would examine other determinants of the region's security, such as economic development, that affect the internal stability of the region's states. An important issue largely ignored by the Moscow-initiated working groups is energy and its impact on the region's stability. For example, securing the safe flow of oil is of paramount interest not only to consumer states but also to Middle East states. Interruption may induce external intervention, which would diminish the sovereignty of the region's states. Another issue that should be on the MECSF agenda is demography: population growth and immigration pose a growing danger to regional stability. Thus, the nonmilitary dimensions of Middle East security would figure prominently in MECSF discussions and activities.

Finally, because the MECSF would be run by the region's states rather than by external cosponsors, participants would enjoy greater freedom to determine their group's membership. As such, the founders may choose to invite all the region's states and to decide whether or not there will be conditions for membership. If they decide to set conditions, the founders would also be able to determine what these conditions should be, through what process they might be formulated and adopted, and how compliance with these conditions should be verified.

Once the ACRS process matures to the point where the sponsors' contribution is no longer essential, and once significant countries in the region that are not parties to the ACRS process join the MECSF, the orchestration of regionwide CSBMs and other arms control measures initiated by ACRS could be transferred to the MECSF. At that point, MECSF members might also determine the relationship between the MECSF and extraregional countries. For example, they may choose to grant some of these countries observer status in MECSF meetings and activities. They would also have to formulate the best manner of ensuring that arrangements and limitations adopted by MECSF members would be respected by these extraregional powers as well.

In the event that significant countries in or outside the Middle East would decline the obligations entailed in joining the MECSF and continue to pose threats to regional stability, the states representing "the new Middle East" should combine their efforts to resist these threats through collective security mechanisms. Such activities would be based on Article VII of the UN Charter, which allows "action with respect to threats to the peace, breaches of the peace, and acts of aggression." The main purpose of the collective security framework would be to deter and to defend against threats to the region's states. Thus, states may choose to consider an attack on any member of the framework as a challenge to all its members. Moreover, defensive measures currently adopted by individual states could be placed at the disposal of the collective security framework, which would reduce the likelihood that they would be regarded as threatening. Indeed, the proposed MECSF as well as the fallback collective security framework would contribute to stability by reducing the propensity of the region's states to take unilateral measures against perceived threats.

America's Continued Engagement

Since the Second World War, U.S. involvement in the Middle East has played a major role in stabilizing the region, and America's engagement will remain a central factor affecting the security of the region for the foreseeable future. Hence, this continued engagement in various facets of the region's affairs should be encouraged.

Serving America's interests in the Middle East, U.S. policies have had a variety of stabilizing effects on the region at large, including

- Facilitating Arab–Israeli negotiations by mediation, by acting as an "honest broker," and by insisting that there is no substitute for face-to-face talks.
- Encouraging a multilateral effort to address the region's pressing problems: economic development, refugees, water resources, the environment, and weapons proliferation. America's role as a prime sponsor of these talks was essential to any gains made in the development of frameworks for solving the problems.
- Deterring radical regimes from engaging in international terrorism and from posing serious threats to the security and survival of the region's moderate states.
- Entering into various forms of strategic cooperation with the region's moderate governments in order to increase their capacity to deter and defend themselves against external threats.
- Transferring military hardware and technologies to moderate govern-

ments, which increased their capacity to defend themselves against radical neighbors.

- Limiting the transfer of technology and material to the region's "rogue regimes" to prevent them from developing or obtaining mass destruction weapons and the capacity to deliver these weapons to neighboring states and more-distant targets.
- Providing economic assistance aimed at reducing deprivation. The resulting improved economic conditions may diminish the extent to which the lower strata among the region's states would seek to relieve their misery in extremist movements.
- Promoting measured democratization, human rights, and free enterprise, as well as a vibrant middle class and a business community that encourage policies to increase economic prosperity—not conflict and war.

The combined impact of these policies contributed to the gradual evolution of a new Middle East—transforming the region from a realm of violence to an arena of negotiations and conflict resolution. Indeed, it is difficult to see how Arab–Israeli peacemaking could have advanced without the cumulative moderating effects of U.S. policies in the region. In the future as well, U.S. continuous commitment to the security of the region's moderate governments and forces will be essential to ensuring stability in the Middle East. Indeed, should the proposal presented here be adopted and a Middle East Cooperative Security Framework be created to complement the states' pursuit of national security, the United States should take part in this new framework as an active associate member.

Thus, the final suggestion is that the United States should remain engaged in the Middle East and that it continue to pursue policies that enhance the region's stability. U.S. efforts in the region have registered significant gains, notably the impressive progress made in Arab–Israeli peacemaking. Washington should not abandon its successful policies in favor of less-certain pursuits.

Conclusions

Bridging the gap between Arab and Israeli threat perceptions and security concerns as well as between their respective approaches to arms control and to national and regional security requires a web of activities pursued at a number of different levels simultaneously. First, a concerted effort must be made to change the perceptions and approaches of Middle East states so that they cease adopting security policies that diminish the security of their neighbors. For this purpose, greater awareness must be developed by the region's states regarding the "security dilemma"—that their neighbors' diminished security rarely translates to gains in their own well-being. Insecure neighbors take steps to address their weaknesses and these steps may diminish regional security. Therefore, if possible, the region's states should pursue policies aimed at enhancing their security without diminishing their neighbors' self-confidence.

Second, every possible effort must be made to enhance the ACRS process. The web of confidence- and security-building measures negotiated in the framework of these talks—including the establishment of a Regional Security Center—should be implemented without delay. The smooth functioning of these measures over time will gradually create an infrastructure of mutual trust that is essential for the eventual negotiations and implementation of more significant arms reduction measures. At the same time initial discussions regarding the conditions and modalities for implementing structural arms control measures should be woven into the ACRS talks. This should be done carefully and in a balanced fashion, without singling out any particular type of weapon.

Third, channels of track-II discussions must be expanded to complement the ACRS process. These channels provide important opportunities for informal exchanges, allowing the parties to air their perceptions and concerns in an uncommitted fashion. Within the framework of these talks, options for overcoming obstacles and resolving deadlocks can be examined in a less charged atmosphere than that sometimes characterizing bilateral and multilateral track-I negotiations.

Fourth, a Middle East Cooperative Security Framework (MECSF) should be established. This framework would gradually replace the ACRS process. It would enjoy a high profile, thus illustrating that the region's states have moved from a narrow pursuit of national security to a serious effort to enhance regional security. It would be managed by the region's states, which would demonstrate that the Middle East peace process has matured. Also, it would combat mythmaking and engage in conflict resolution in order to diminish the danger that the peace process might be reversed.

Finally, the United States must remain engaged in the Middle East and must continue to pursue the array of its present policies in the region. By facilitating the peaceful resolution of disputes, by helping deter aggression and extremism, by encouraging economic development, democratization, and human rights, and by strengthening moderate governments in the region, the United States should continue to enhance the region's security.

Taken together, these five measures comprise an architecture for security building in the Middle East. If considered carefully and implemented wisely, these measures can significantly enhance the region's stability. Pursuing these measures would present the region's leaders with a difficult challenge requiring much sophistication and finesse. If they accept the challenge, the reward may be a new, more secure Middle East.

Appendix A

Remarks by Secretary of State James A. Baker, III, before the Organizational Meeting for Multilateral Negotiations on the Middle East, House of Unions, January 28, 1992

Foreign Minister Kozyrev, Distinguished Delegates:

Less than three months ago, history was made in Madrid. There, in an unprecedented gathering, Israel and its Arab neighbors sat directly across the table from one another. Immediately after, bilateral negotiations began: between Israel and Lebanon, Israel and Syria, and Israel and a joint Jordanian-Palestinian delegation.

We have now witnessed three rounds of bilateral negotiations in as many months. In every case, the parties are engaging on substantive issues. And even when the parties are seemingly bogged down in procedural wrangles, they are for the most part the ones who are sorting them out, resolving their problems in face-to-face negotiations.

I do not mean to suggest we are satisfied with all that has transpired or naive about the hurdles and challenges that lie ahead. As I said in Madrid, we must crawl before we can walk and we must walk before we can run. We are not running, and there are those who would say that we are not even walking. But we are moving, and that is key, for all potentially good ideas and formulas for peace count for little in the absence of an agreed-upon process to engage them. And such a process of direct engagement—a process designed to lead to comprehensive peace on the basis of United Nations Security Council Resolutions 242 and 338—is now well under way.

We meet here today in newly independent and newly democratic Russia. I find it hard to imagine any setting being more fitting. As recently as a few years ago, few would have even dared to dream that Russia would be going through the profound transformation we are now witnessing. This should tell us something; simply put, where there is vision and where there is courage, there is also possibility and promise.

We have gathered to explore new possibilities for the Middle East. As you all know, the invitation to the Madrid conference stated that those parties who wished to attend multilateral negotiations would convene two weeks after the opening of the conference to organize those negotiations. Well, I am afraid we are a bit late. But it is my hope—and it should be our determination—that what we are embarking upon today will prove to have been well worth waiting for.

What is it that we are here to begin? We are here to organize ourselves in preparation for a process that with time will address issues common to all the peoples of the Middle East. Despite the political issues that currently divide governments and peoples, there are real ties that bind the peoples of the Middle East together. They breathe the same air, drink the same water, are vulnerable to the same diseases, and have all suffered from the very tragic costs of war.

It is for these reasons that we have come together—to address those issues that are common to the region and that do not necessarily respect national or geographic boundaries. These issues can best be addressed by the concerted efforts of regional parties together with the support of the international community and the resources and expertise that it can provide.

Let me take this opportunity to make something clear. What we are embarking upon here in Moscow is in no way a substitute for what we are trying to promote in the bilateral negotiations. Only the bilateral talks can address and one day resolve the basic issues of territory, security and peace which the parties have identified as the core elements of a lasting and comprehensive peace between Israel and its Arab neighbors.

But it is also true that these bilateral negotiations do not take place in a vacuum, and that the condition of the region at large will affect them. In short, the multilateral talks are intended as a complement to the bilateral negotiations; each can and will buttress the other.

This is true for three reasons. First, multilateral negotiations on regional issues will send a powerful signal that all parties are unequivocally committed to peace and reconciliation.

Second, multilateral negotiations on regional issues will address on their own merits a range of regional problems crying out for resolution. There are pressing human problems—poverty, refugees, disease, and above all, the danger of war—that need to be addressed. It would be tragic and irresponsible to put these problems of real and profound human need on hold while waiting for peace to come.

Third, multilateral negotiations on regional issues can begin to improve the lives of people and create a basis for greater stability in the area. As progress is made, as tangible benefits emerge, a vision of what real peace might mean will also begin to emerge.

Today, we will be hearing statements by delegations from the region and from others outside the region. I would hope that everyone would take advantage of this opportunity to discuss how we can best approach the challenges common to all who live or have a stake in the well-being of the Middle East.

Tomorrow, we move from the conference hall to working groups where the important task of organizing the discrete groups and determining how they will proceed will begin. The regional parties will have the primary responsibility for setting the agendas. The cosponsors, along with the international community, are prepared to play an active supporting role. I would like to say just a few words about each of the five groups.

First, economic development. For too long, the substantial human, natural, and financial resources of the Middle East have not been utilized to their full potential. Military spending has crowded out development; intraregional trade and investment has remained small; and external assistance flows have cultivated dependency more than growth.

An economic development working group could begin to consider how this picture could be turned around by: (1) focusing the attention of interested parties on the urgent economic needs of the West Bank and Gaza; (2) assessing and considering job-creating regional infrastructure projects in energy, communications and transportation; (3) looking into the development of trade as an engine of economic growth and job creation; and (4) exploring the potential for expanding tourism in a climate of peace. We urge regional parties to be creative as they shape an appropriate work plan for this group.

Second, the environment. From groundwater contamination to oil spills, Middle Eastern countries face daunting environmental challenges which are mounting daily under the twin pressures of population growth and industrialization.

Initially, an environment working group could be the catalyst for the exchange of scientific findings on the extent of shared environmental problems. The Gulf of Aqaba might be a good place to start.

Over time, the group could expand to explore parallel or joint projects on the region's common problems, ranging from preservation of archeological sites to waste disposal. Again, the agenda could be as expansive as the regional parties define.

Third, water. Ensuring reliable supplies of this precious resource is a fundamental security—as well as economic—challenge to all the regional parties, especially in the arid, drought-prone conditions of the Middle East.

A water working group could begin to explore the dimensions of this challenge, beginning with seminars to exchange forecasts of demand and available supply and leading over time to cooperative activities in the areas of water pricing and allocation policies, desalination techniques, and reuse of brackish water. Interested extraregional parties could share expertise, technologies and resources.

Fourth, is the issue of refugees. Almost all of the conflicts that punctuate the history of the Middle East have been the occasion of a substantial number of individuals leaving their homes. Often, they have had to live for months or years in temporary, crowded camps. This experience is common to all too many of the region's peoples. It is not our objective to ascribe cause or attribute responsibility for the refugee problem. Rather, it is to see whether the parties of this region, helped by states from outside, can provide needed resources to improve the lot of these men, women, and children.

Finally, arms control and regional security. The Gulf War was a vivid reminder of just how destructive patterns of arms acquisition and production have and can become—undermining the very security they were intended to promote. An arms control working group could begin to tackle this issue, but in a way that recognizes the vital security interests at stake for all the parties of the region.

In the first instance, we envision offering the regional parties our thinking about potential approaches to arms control, drawing upon a vast reservoir of experience stemming from attempts to regulate military competition in Europe and other regions. From this base, the group might move forward to considering a set of modest confidence-building or transparency measures covering notifications of selected military-related activities and crisis-prevention communications. The purpose would be to lessen the prospects for incidents and miscalculation that could lead to heightened competition or even conflict.

In our view, and again, based upon our own experience with arms control, we believe such an approach offers the best chance for success. At the same time, we would not discourage or rule out efforts to decrease the level of militarization, especially involving those systems most likely to contribute to instability amidst crises. Eventually, and as called for by President Bush's 1991 initiative, we would hope to see the level of conventional arms reaching the region greatly diminished and weapons of mass destruction eliminated.

Let me close with one thought. We live in an age when many of the world's regions, once ravaged by war, are now coming together. We see this above all here in Europe, but we see it too in Asia and in Central and Latin America. The results are obvious: peace and security, prosperity, better quality of life. Increasingly, the Middle East stands out, but not in the way that should make any of us proud. Our challenge—our opportunity—is to begin the process of making the Middle East a region, not just in the geographic sense, but in the political, the economic, and, indeed, in the human sense as well.

This gathering here today reflects the commitment and resources of those outside the region who want to assist in this effort. The cosponsors, the United States together with Russia, strongly encourage the parties in the region for whom this process offers real benefits, to engage promptly and fully. This is a rare opportunity; do not let it pass by.

Appendix B

Statement on Arms Control and Regional Security

Preamble

The regional participants in the Arms Control and Regional Security working group, Reaffirming their respect for the Charter of the United Nations,

Bearing in mind the urgent necessity of achieving a just, lasting, and comprehensive peace settlement in the Middle East based on United Nations Security Council Resolutions 242 and 338, and conscious of the historic breakthroughs toward such a settlement since the 1991 Madrid Middle East Peace Conference, particularly the Israeli-Palestinian Declaration of Principles and the subsequent Agreement on the Gaza and Jericho Area, and the Jordan-Israel Peace Treaty of October 26, 1994,

Agreeing that all regional parties should pursue the common purpose of achieving full and lasting relations of peace, openness, mutual confidence, security, stability, and cooperation throughout the region,

Recognizing that the multilateral working groups, including the Arms Control and Regional Security working group, should continue to complement the bilateral negotiations and help improve the climate for resolving the core issues at the heart of the Middle East peace process, and that the peace process also created the opportunity to cooperate in addressing additional issues of regionwide concern,

Embarking in this context on a process through the Arms Control and Regional Security working group to establish arms control and regional security arrangements aimed at safeguarding the region from the dangers and ominous consequences of future wars and the horrors of mass destruction, and enabling all possible resources to be devoted to the welfare of the peoples of the region, including such areas as economic and social development,

Recognizing the importance of preventing the proliferation of nuclear, chemical, and biological weapons and of preventing the excessive accumulation of conventional arms in enhancing international and regional peace and security,

Conscious that the arms control and regional security process seeks to achieve a stable balance among military capabilities in the region that takes into account quantitative and qualitative factors, and also recognizes the significance of structural factors, and that provides for equal security for all,

Welcoming the special role of the United States and Russia as active cosponsors of the Middle East peace process and calling on them and other extraregional states to provide continuing support for the objectives and arrangements of the arms control and regional security process,

Recognizing that the full realization of the objectives contained in this Statement would be facilitated by the involvement in the arms control and regional security process of all regional parties, and calling on all such parties to support the principles contained in this Statement and, in this connection, to join the arms control and regional security process at an early date,

Have adopted the following:

I. Fundamental Principles Governing Security Relations Among Regional Participants in the Arms Control and Regional Security Working Group

In their pursuit of a just, lasting and comprehensive peace in the Middle East, the regional participants will be governed in their security policies by the following fundamental principles, among others:

- The participants reaffirm their commitment to the principles of the Charter of the United Nations

- Participants must refrain from the threat or use of force and from acts of terrorism and subversion.
- Security requires that participants fulfill in good faith obligations under international law.
- Security must be based on respect for and acknowledgment of sovereignty, territorial integrity, and political independence, noninterference in internal affairs, and reconciliation and cooperation among participants.
- Arms control and regional security arrangements should be aimed at achieving equal security for all at the lowest possible level of armaments and military forces.
- Military means, while needed to fulfill the inherent right of self-defense, and to discourage aggression, cannot by themselves provide security.

Enduring security requires the peaceful resolution of conflicts in the region and the promotion of good neighborly relations and common interests.

II. Guidelines for the Middle East Arms Control and Regional Security Process

The regional participants recognize the following as guidelines for the arms control and regional security process:

- The arms control and regional security process, as an integral part of the Middle East peace process, should create a favorable climate for progress in the bilateral negotiations and complement them by developing tangible measures in parallel with progress in the bilateral talks.
- The arms control and regional security process should strive to enhance security and general stability on a regionwide basis, even beyond the scope of the Arab-Israeli conflict, by pursuing regional security and arms control measures that reduce tension or the risk of war.
- The scope of the process must be comprehensive, covering a broad range of regional security, confidence- and security-building and arms-control measures that address all threats to security and all categories of arms and weapons systems.

- The arms control and regional security process should not at any stage diminish the security of any individual state or give a state a military advantage over any other.
- The basic framework of the process is to pursue a determined, step-by-step approach which sets ambitious goals and proceeds toward them in a realistic way.
- The basis for decision making on each issue in the arms control and regional security process should be consensus by the regional participants directly concerned.
- Each regional arrangement adopted in the arms control and regional security process should be the result of direct regional negotiations and should be implemented by all those regional parties relevant to the arrangement.
- Strict compliance with arms control and disarmament measures adopted within the framework of the arms control and regional security process is essential to the integrity of that process and for building confidence among the regional participants.
- All arms control and disarmament measures adopted by regional participants within the framework of the arms control and regional security process will be effectively verifiable by the regional parties themselves and should include, where appropriate, mutual on-site inspection and other rigorous monitoring techniques and mechanisms, and such verification could be complementary with verification measures in international arrangements.

III. Statements of Intent on Objectives for the Arms Control and Regional Security Process

In the context of achieving a just, secure, comprehensive, and lasting peace and reconciliation, the regional participants agree to pursue, inter alia, the following arms control and regional security objectives:

- preventing conflicts from occurring through misunderstanding or miscalculation by adopting confidence- and security-building measures that increase transparency and openness and reduce the risk of surprise attack and by developing regional institutional arrangements that enhance security and the process of arms control;

- limiting military spending in the region so that additional resources can be made available to other areas such as economic and social development;
- reducing stockpiles of conventional arms and preventing a conventional arms race in the region as part of an effort to provide enhanced security at lower levels of armaments and militarization, to reduce the threat of large-scale destruction posed by such weapons, and to move toward force structures that do not exceed legitimate defense requirements;
- promoting cooperation among regional participants in the peaceful uses of outer space, including the pursuit of appropriate means of sharing the benefits from satellite systems, of ensuring that outer space and other environments will not be used for acts of aggression by regional participants, and of enhancing the security of regional participants; and
- (language proposed by Israel) establishing the Middle East as a mutually verifiable zone free of nuclear, chemical, biological weapons and ballistic missiles in view of their high destructive capacity and their potential to promote instability in the region.
- (language proposed by the United States) establishing the Middle East as a zone free of all weapons of mass destruction, including nuclear, chemical, and biological weapons and their delivery systems—since such weapons, with their high destructive capacity and their potential to promote instability in the region, pose a grave threat to security—through a combination of regional arrangements, such as weapons-free zones, and international arrangements, such as the BWC, the NPT, and the CWC.
- (language proposed by Egypt) establishing a zone free of all weapons of mass destruction, including nuclear, chemical, and biological weapons and their delivery systems, since such weapons, with their high destructive capacity and their potential to exacerbate the arms race in the region, pose the greatest threat to its security.
that all parties of the region will adhere to the NPT in the near future.

Regional participants will be guided in their conduct by the principles embodied in this Statement and will refrain from actions or activities that are inconsistent with its guidelines or principles and that preclude the attainment of its objectives.

Abbreviations

ACDA—US Arms Control and Disarmament Agency
ACRS—Arms control and regional security
BMDO—Ballistic Missile Defense Organization
BWC—Biological Weapons Convention
CFE—Conventional Armed Forces in Europe
CSBM—confidence- and security-building measure
CSCE—Conference on Security and Cooperation in Europe (see OSCE)
CWC—Chemical Weapons Convention
DOP—Declaration of Principles
IAEA—International Atomic Energy Agency
IAS—incidents at sea
INF—Intermediate-range nuclear forces
MBFR—Mutual and balanced force reduction
MECSF—Middle East Cooperative Security Framework
NPT—Non-Proliferation Treaty
NWFZ—nuclear weapon-free zone
OSCE—Organization for Security and Cooperation in Europe (before 1 January 1995 called the Conference on Security and Cooperation in Europe [CSCE]).
RSC—regional security center
SALT—Strategic Arms Limitation Talks
SAR—search and rescue
START—Strategic Arms Reduction Talks/Treaty
WMDFZ—Weapons-of-mass-destruction–free zone

—

Glossary

Biological Weapons Convention (BWC): Prohibits the development, production, and stockpiling of bacteriological (biological) and toxin weapons and mandates their destruction. Signed on 10 April 1972; entered into force on 26 March 1975.

Chemical Weapons Convention (CWC): Prohibits the development, production, stockpiling, and use of chemical weapons and mandates their destruction. Opened for signature on 13 January 1993; enters into force in April 1997.

compellence: A strategy of using a threat to persuade an opponent to perform some desired action.

confrontation states: In the Arab–Israeli conflict the confrontation states have been the states adjacent to Israel; mainly Egypt, Jordan, Syria and Lebanon.

deception, military: Actions executed to mislead foreign decision makers, causing them to derive and accept desired appreciations of military capabilities, intentions, operations, or other activities that evoke foreign actions that contribute to the originator's objectives. There are three categories of military deception: (1) strategic military deception—Military deception planned and executed to result in foreign national policies and actions which support the originator's national objectives, policies, and strategic military plans; (2) tactical military deception—Military deception planned and executed by and in support of operational commanders against the pertinent threat to result in opposing operational actions favorable to the originator's plans and operations; (3) Department/service military deception—Military deception planned and executed by Military Services about military systems, doctrine, tactics, techniques, personnel or service operations, or other activities to result in for-

Sources: U.S. Department of Defense, *Dictionary of Military Terms* (Mechanicsburg, PA: Stackpole Books, 1995). Descriptions of conventions and treaties are from Stockholm International Peace Research Institute, *SIPRI Yearbook 1995: Armaments, Disarmament and International Security* (New York: Oxford University Press, 1995).

eign actions which increase or maintain the originator's capabilities relative to adversaries.

defense in depth: The siting of mutually supporting defense positions designed to absorb and progressively weaken attack, prevent initial observations of the whole position of the enemy, and allow the commander to maneuver his reserve.

deterrence: A strategy of using a threat to dissuade an opponent from attempting to achieve an objective.

  extended deterrence: The attempt to prevent a military attack against an ally by threatening retaliation.

  strategic deterrence: A strategy of using threat (nuclear, biological, chemical) to dissuade an opponent from attempting to achieve his objectives.

division: A major administrative and tactical unit formation that combines in itself the necessary arms and services required for sustained combat. It is larger than a regiment/brigade and smaller than a corps. Divisions could be armored, containing main battle tanks, or mechanized, containing more infantry and armored fighting vehicles.

doctrine: Fundamental principles by which the military forces or elements thereof guide their actions in support of national objectives.

echelon: A fraction of a command in the direction of depth to which a principal combat mission is assigned; i.e., attack echelon (first echelon), support echelon (second echelon), reserve echelon (third echelon).

extended deterrence: *See* deterrence.

force structure: *See* military capability.

full-scope safeguards: Measures applied and supervised by the International Atomic Energy Agency (IAEA) to ensure that states signatory to the Nuclear Non-Proliferation Treaty abide by the articles of the treaty—thereby preventing the diversion of any type of nuclear material to nuclear weapons—and that nuclear material and specified equipment will be exported to nonnuclear weapon states only under IAEA safeguards.

Geneva Protocol: Prohibits the use in war of asphyxiating, poisonous, or other gases, and of bacteriological methods of warfare. Signed on 17 June 1925; in force on 8 February 1928.

Intermediate-range Nuclear Forces (INF) Treaty: Obliges the parties to destroy all land-based missiles with a range of 500–5,500 km and their launchers by 1 June 1991. Signed by the United States and the USSR at Washington, D.C., on 8 December 1987; entered into force on 1 June 1988.

low-intensity conflict: Political-military confrontation between contending states or groups below conventional war and above the routine, peaceful competition among states.

mechanized division: *See* division.

Middle East nuclear weapon-free zone: Proposed by the shah of Iran in 1974 because of the rapid diffusion of nuclear technology in the region. Egypt subsequently cosponsored the proposal, which was passed as a resolution by the

United Nations General Assembly (UNGA) 128–0, with Israel and Burma abstaining. In October 1980 Israel submitted a separate draft NWFZ resolution to the UN. Since then, the UNGA has passed such a resolution annually. While the resolution does not define a zone, Egypt has said that all concerned parties should be included, at a minimum the Arab states, Israel, and Iran. A 1990 UN study endorsed this definition, extending the zone as far as Libya to the west. In 1991 another such resolution was passed; Israel voted for it but called for direct negotiations. The IAEA has produced two reports on applications of safeguards to the Middle East. The UNGA again adopted the resolution in 1993.

military capability: The ability to achieve a specified wartime objective (win a war or battle or destroy a target set). It includes four major components: force structure, modernization, readiness, and sustainability. (1) Force structure— Numbers, size, and composition of the units that comprise defense forces; e.g., divisions, ships, and airwings. (2) Modernization—Technical sophistication of forces, units, weapon systems, and equipment. (3) Readiness—The ability of forces, units, weapons systems, or equipment to deliver the outputs for which they were designed (includes the ability to deploy and employ without unacceptable delays). (4) Sustainability—The ability to maintain the necessary level and duration of operational activity to achieve military objectives. Sustainability is a function of providing for and maintaining those levels of ready forces, materiel, and consumables necessary to support military effort.

military objectives: The derived set of military actions to be taken to implement National Command Authorities guidance in support of national objectives. Defines the results to be achieved by the military and assigns tasks to commanders.

military posture: The military disposition, strength, and condition of readiness as they affect capabilities.

national military strategy: The art and science of distributing and applying military power to attain national objectives in peace and war.

national security: A collective term encompassing both national defense and foreign relations. Specifically, the condition provided by (1) a military or defense advantage over any foreign nation or group of nations, or (2) a favorable foreign relations position, or (3) a defense posture capable of successfully resisting hostile or destructive action from within or without, overt or covert.

national security interests: The foundation for the development of valid national objectives that define national goals or purposes. National security interests include preserving political identity, framework, and institutions; fostering economic well-being; and bolstering international order supporting vital national interests.

national technical means: Measures that countries can use independently, for example, satellite monitoring, to verify compliance to arms control treaties, as opposed to multilateral and bilateral means.

Non-Proliferation Treaty (NPT): Prohibits the transfer by nuclear weapon states to any recipient whatsoever of nuclear weapons or other nuclear explosive devices or of control over them, as well as the assistance, encouragement, or inducement of any nonnuclear weapon state to manufacture or otherwise acquire such weapons or devices. Prohibits the receipt by nonnuclear weapon states of any transfer whatsoever, as well as the manufacture or other acquisition by those states, of nuclear weapons or other nuclear explosive devices. Nonnuclear weapon states undertake to conclude safeguard agreements with the International Atomic Energy Agency with a view to preventing diversion of nuclear energy from peaceful uses to nuclear weapons or other nuclear explosive devices. Signed on 1 July 1968; in force on 5 March 1970.

Open Skies Treaty: The treaty obliges the parties to submit their territories to short-notice unarmed surveillance flights. The area of application stretches from Vancouver, Canada, eastward to Vladivostock, Russia. The Open Skies Treaty was negotiated between the member states of the Warsaw Treaty Organization (WTO) and NATO. Signed on 24 March 1992; not yet in force.

operational arms control: Efforts to prevent war by misunderstanding or miscalculation, to reduce the possibility of surprise attack, and ultimately to diminish the use of force.

operational level of war: The level of war at which campaigns and major operations are planned, conducted, and sustained to accomplish strategic objectives within theaters or areas of operations. Activities at this level link tactics and strategy by establishing operational objectives needed to accomplish the strategic objectives, sequencing events to achieve the operational objectives, initiating actions, and applying resources to bring about and sustain these events. These activities imply a broader dimension of time or space than do tactics; they ensure the logistic and administrative support of tactical forces, and provide the means by which tactical successes are exploited to achieve strategic objectives. *See also* strategic level of war; tactical level of war.

order of battle: The identification, strength, command structure, and disposition of the personnel, units, and equipment of any military force.

Outer Space Treaty: Governs the activities of states in the exploration and use of outer space, including the moon and other celestial bodies. The treaty prohibits the placing into orbit around the earth of any objects carrying nuclear weapons or any other kinds of weapons of mass destruction. Signed on 27 January 1967; in force on 10 October 1967.

prepositioning: To place military units, equipment, or supplies at or near the point of planned use or at a designated location to reduce reaction time, and to ensure timely support of a specific force during initial phases of an operation.

security assurances: A negative security assurance is a commitment by nuclear weapon states not to use or threaten to use nuclear weapons against nonnuclear weapon states. A positive security assurance is a commitment by nuclear weapon states to provide assistance to any nonnuclear weapon state (party to the NPT) that is a victim of an act of aggression or an object of a threat of aggression in which nuclear weapons are used.

South Pacific Nuclear Free Zone Treaty (Treaty of Rarotonga): Prohibits the manufacture or acquisition by other means of any nuclear explosive device, as well as possession or control over such device by the parties anywhere inside or outside the area as described in an annex. The parties also undertake not to supply nuclear material or equipment unless subject to IAEA safeguards and to prevent in their territories the stationing as well as the testing of any nuclear explosive device. Each party remains free to allow visits, as well as transit, by foreign ships and aircraft. Signed at Rarotonga, Cook Islands, on 6 August 1985; in force on 11 December 1986.

START I Treaty: Requires the United States and Russia to make phased reductions in their offensive strategic nuclear forces over a seven-year period. Signed on 31 July 1991; in force on 5 December 1994. The START II Treaty further reduces and limits strategic offensive arms. Signed on 3 January 1993; not in force as of 1 May 1996.

strategic advantage: The overall relative power relationship of opponents that enables one nation or group of nations effectively to control the course of a military/political situation.

strategic deterrence: *See* deterrence.

strategic level of war: The level of war at which a nation, often as a member of a group of nations, determines national or multinational (alliance or coalition) security objectives and guidance, and develops and uses national resources to accomplish these objectives. Activities at this level establish national and multinational military objectives; sequence initiatives; define limits and assess risks for the use of military and other instruments of national power; develop global plans or theater war plans to achieve these objectives; and provide military forces and other capabilities in accordance with strategic plans. *See also* operational level of war; tactical level of war.

strategic vulnerability: The susceptibility of vital elements of national power to being seriously decreased or adversely changed by the application of actions within the capability of another nation to impose. Strategic vulnerability may pertain to political, geographic, economic, scientific, societal, or military factors.

structural arms control: Reductions in military manpower as well as conventional and unconventional (nuclear, chemical, and biological) weapons, ultimately producing major force reductions.

tactical depth: A geographic area in which military tactical units can maneuver.

tactical level of war: The level of war at which battles and engagements are planned and executed to accomplish military objectives assigned to tactical units or task forces. Activities at this level focus on the ordered arrangement and maneuver of combat elements in relation to each other and to the enemy to achieve combat objectives. *See also* operational level of war; strategic level of war.

track-I talks: Formal negotiations between governments.

track-II talks: Informal talks between institutions or individuals not connected to governments.

transparency: A term associated with military confidence- and security-building measures. By the exchange of military information and the prenotification of military exercises by either side, the aim is to increase predictability, to prevent war from any misunderstanding or miscalculation, and also to reduce the possibility of surprise attack.

Treaty on Conventional Armed Forces in Europe (CFE Treaty): Sets ceilings on five categories of military equipment (battle tanks, armored combat vehicles, artillery pieces, combat aircraft, and attack helicopters) in an area stretching from the Atlantic Ocean to the Ural Mountains (ATTU zone). The treaty was negotiated and signed by the member states of the Warsaw Treaty Organization (WTO) and NATO within the framework of the Conference on Security and Cooperation in Europe (CSCE). Signed on 19 November 1990; in force on 9 November 1992.

Treaty of Tlatelolco: Prohibits nuclear weapons in Latin America and the Caribbean. Prohibits the testing, use, manufacture, production, or acquisition by any means, as well as receipt, storage, installation, deployment, and any form of possession of any nuclear weapons by Latin American countries. The parties should conclude agreements with the International Atomic Energy Agency for the application of safeguards to their nuclear activities. Signed at Mexico City on 14 February 1967; entered into force on 22 April 1968; modified and amended in 1990, 1991, and 1992.

verification: In arms control, any action, including inspection, detection, and identification, taken to ascertain compliance with agreed measures.

weapons of mass destruction: In arms control usage, weapons that are capable of a high order of destruction and/or of being used in such a manner as to destroy large numbers of people. Weapons of mass destruction can be nuclear, chemical, biological, and radiological weapons. The means of transporting or propelling the weapon, where such means is a separable and divisible part of the weapon, are excluded.

Index

Abu Musa island, 59

ACDA. *See* Arms Control and Disarmament Agency

ACRS. *See* Arms Control and Regional Security talks

"Agreements of Friendship and Cooperation," 41

Airborne Warning and Control System (AWACS), 48

aircraft: F-15 and F-16, 48, 68; MiG-21 and MiG-23, 51

Al-Ahram, 23

Algeria, 22, 45

Al-Ra'y, 23

American Academy of Arts and Sciences, 88

American Association for the Advancement of Science, 88

Amir, Yig'al, 67

Amman, Jordan, 38

antitactical ballistic missiles, 30

Arab League, 2, 44–45, 47; economic boycott of Israel, 51; oil embargo, 50; Pact of the League of Arab States, 47; security recommendations, 85–86

Arab media, 23

Arab nationalism, 23

Arab Organization for Industry (AOI), 48

Arab Organization for Military Industries, 48

Arab states, 33–72; "Agreements of Friendship and Cooperation," 41; approaches to arms control, 61–66; arms supplies, 47–48; collective security, 70; cultural autonomy, 12; grand strategy, 46–53; Israeli perception of, 7–12; oil embargo, 50; security concerns, 74–76; security environment, 53–61; security perceptions, 34–46; security policy, 66–71; security threats, 63–69; and Soviet Union, 41–42; strategic vulnerability, 37–38, 47–50. *See also specific states*

Arafat, Yasir, 3, 21, 53

armed peace, 57, 66

arms control: Arab approaches to, 61–66; bilateral and multilateral levels, 62–66; Conference on Disarmament, 27–28; Israeli approach, 26–28; multilateral, 70; nuclear, 82–84; operational, 4, 63, 114; policy of diversification of supplies, 47–48; structural, 115; verification,

116; visionary goals for, 80. *See also specific weapons*

Arms Control and Disarmament Agency (ACDA), 2

Arms Control and Regional Security (ACRS) talks, 21, 63–64, 81–82, 100–101; conceptual basket, 5, 81; CSBM negotiations, 81; fundamental principles, 104–5; future process phases, 86–87; guidelines, 105–6; objectives, 106–7; operational basket, 5, 81; process, 4–6, 64; process enhancement, 80–82, 95; statement on Arms Control and Regional Security, 5–6, 64, 81, 86, 103–7

Arrow missile, 30, 41

Assad, Hafez el-, 19

ATBMs (antitactical ballistic missiles), 30

attrition, war of, 10, 49

autonomy, cultural, 12

AWACS (Airborne Warning and Control System), 48

Aziz, Tarik, 39

Bab-el-Mandeb, 42

Baker, James A. III, 20, 39; remarks before Organizational Meeting for Multilateral Negotiations on the Middle East, 97–101

Balfour Declaration, 37

Ballistic Missile Defense Organization (BMDO), 15, 30, 41

ballistic missiles, 68; Arrow, 30, 41; Iraqi, 25; Jericho-IIB, 39, 68; no-Dong, 25; over-the-horizon threats, 29; war of the cities (Iran–Iraq war), 43

battle, order of, 17, 114

Begin, Menachem, 13

Bekaa valley, 38

Ben Gurion, David, 8–9, 14

biological weapons, 11, 25

Biological Weapons Convention (BWC), 27, 65, 111

BMDO (Ballistic Missile Defense Organization), 15, 30, 41

borders: clashes, 60–61; defensible, 18, 49

boycott: economic, 51; intellectual, 23

Britain. *See* United Kingdom

Bush, George, 63

BWC (Biological Weapons Convention), 27, 65, 111

Camp David Accords, 50–51

Carnegie Corporation, 88

Carnegie Endowment for International Peace, 88

Central Intelligence Agency (CIA), 2

CFE treaty (Conventional Armed Forces in Europe treaty), 82, 116

chemical weapons, 11, 25, 43, 45

Chemical Weapons Convention (CWC), 27, 65, 111

Chinese missile boats, 59

Christians, 15

CIA, 2

Cold War, 19–20

collective security, 70–71

compellance, 37, 111

Comprehensive Test Ban Treaty (CTBT), 65–66

Conference on Disarmament, 27–28

Conference on Security and Cooperation in Europe (CSCE) Communication Center, 81

Conference on Security and Cooperation in the Middle East (CSCME), 71

confidence- and security-building measures, 5, 56, 69, 75, 80; negotiating, 81; political-military, 5, 63; technical-military, 5, 63

conflict, low-intensity, 112

confrontation states, 111

containment, 58

Conventional Armed Forces in Europe (CFE) treaty, 82, 116

cooperation: "Agreements of Friend-

ship and Cooperation," 41; strategic, 40–41
cooperative security, 66, 71
CSBMs. *See* confidence- and security-building measures
CSCE (Conference on Security and Cooperation in Europe), 81
cultural autonomy, 12
CWC (Chemical Weapons Convention), 27, 65, 111

Damascus, Syria, 38
Damascus Declaration, 60, 70
deception, military, 111–12
Declaration of Principles (DOP), 3, 86
defense: in depth, 29, 112; French-Israeli cooperation, 14
defensible borders, 18, 49
de Gaulle, Charles, 14
deniability, plausible, 17
deterrence, 57, 69–71, 112; Arab concerns, 76; extended, 112; strategic, 15–16, 31, 37, 51, 112
disarmament. *See* arms control
division, 112
doctrine: definition, 112; military, 49, 56–57; strategic parity, 51; weapons of last resort, 66, 68, 74–75
dominance: escalation, 16
DOP (Declaration of Principles), 3, 86

echelon, 29, 112
economic boycott of Israel, 51
economic development, 99–100
Egypt: 1956 assault on, 18; arms supplies, 47–48; Camp David Accords, 50–51; Damascus Declaration, 60, 70; financial aid, 55; Gulf War, 55; Islamic extremism, 22–23; Mubarak government, 22; Suez war, 35; terrorism, 16; 1967 war, 10, 13, 36; 1973 war, 10, 14, 49; 1968 war of attrition, 10, 49
embargo, oil, 50
environment, 100

escalation dominance, 16
Ethiopia, 15
ethnic cleansing, 8
extended deterrence. *See* deterrence

FAFO (Institute for Applied Social Science), 87–88
F-15 aircraft and F-16 aircraft, 48, 68
Fissile Material Cutoff treaty, 65
force structure: Arab, 52, 56, 60, 62, 83; Arab states' view of Israel's f.s., 20, 57, 74, 75; in discussion of arms control, 74, 84, 107; Israeli, 9, 18–19, 29, 31; Israel's view of Arab states' f.s., 21, 77
Ford Foundation, 88
France: arms control, 61; defense agreements, 14, 60
friendship agreements, 41

Gadhafi, Mu'ammar, 19
Gaza, 38
GCC. *See* Gulf Cooperation Council
Geneva Protocol, 112
Goldstein, Baruch, 67
Gorbachev, Mikhail, 19
Great Britain. *See* United Kingdom
Gulf Cooperation Council (GCC), 53; arms supplies, 47–48, 60; defense agreements, 52, 60; and Iraq, 42–43. *See also specific states*
Gulf states, 52–53, 57–61; and Iraq, 42–43. *See also specific states*
Gulf War, 20, 23, 39–40, 44, 53–55

Hamas, 3, 21–22
Hariri, Rafik, 55
Hashemite Kingdom of Jordan: arms supplies, 47–48; military doctrine, 49; as Palestine (myth), 91; peace with Israel, 3, 20, 22, 63; Regional Security Center, 5, 81; strategic vulnerability, 37–38; terrorism, 16; 1967 war, 10, 13, 36; 1973 war, 10, 14, 49

hegemony, 79
Hezbullah, 21–22, 28, 55
Holocaust, 8, 11, 14
Hussein, Saddam, 11, 21, 23–25, 43, 58–59; Gulf War, 39–40

IAEA (International Atomic Energy Agency), 27, 112
IAS (incidents at sea), 81
IDF (Israeli Defense Forces), 8–9; Arab concerns, 75; defense in depth, 29; grand strategy, 13–15, 17–18
incidents at sea, 81
INF (intermediate-range nuclear forces), 82
Institute for Applied Social Science (FAFO), 87–88
Institute on Global Conflict and Cooperation (University of California), 88
Institut Français des Rélations Internationales, 88
intellectual boycott, 23
Intermediate-range Nuclear Forces (INF), 82
Intermediate-range Nuclear Forces (INF) Treaty, 27, 112
International Atomic Energy Agency (IAEA): safeguards, 27, 112
Intifada, 13, 46
Iran, 2, 58–59; Arab concerns, 59–60, 75; ballistic missiles, 25, 29–30; Islamic extremism, 21; nuclear program, 24; rearmament program, 59–60; relations with Israel, 15, 77–78; security recommendations, 85–86; weapons of mass destruction, 25
Iran–Iraq War, 42–43, 53, 57–58
Iraq, 2, 58–59, 71; Arab Gulf states and, 42–43; arms supplies, 47–48; ballistic missiles, 25, 29–30; biological weapons, 25; chemical weapons, 43; Gulf War, 39–40, 44; Iran–Iraq war, 42–43, 53, 57–58; nuclear

weapons, 23–24; Soviet–Iraqi agreement, 41; 1967 war, 10, 13, 36; 1973 war, 49; weapons of mass destruction, 25
Islamic extremism, 21–23
Islamic Jihad, 3, 21
Israel, 7–31; alliances with minorities, 15; alliances with peripheral states, 15; Arab perceptions of, 34–46; Arab response to, 47–50; arms control, 26–28, 30–31, 62, 64–65; arms supplies, 48; Camp David Accords, 50–51; Declaration of Principles, 3, 86; deterrence strategy, 15–16, 31; expansion of, 91; French defense cooperation, 14; grand strategy, 12–19; invasion of Lebanon, 13; isolation of, 51–52; Jewish emigration to, 19; military doctrine, 49, 57; nuclear weapons, 11, 16–17, 39, 77; Ofeq satellite system, 41; order of battle, 17; peace with Jordan, 3, 22, 63; peace with Syria and Lebanon, 3, 31, 54–56, 85; regional environment, 19–25; security, 16, 18; security concerns, 10, 76–78; security perception, 7–12; security policy, 28–31; strategic depth vulnerability, 38; Suez war, 35; Syrian red lines, 15–16; U.S. relations, 14, 20, 35, 40–41; 1948 war, 8, 14; 1967 war, 10, 13–14, 18, 36; 1973 war, 10, 14, 49; war in Lebanon, 51; 1968 war of attrition, 10, 49; weapons of last resort doctrine, 68, 74–75
Israeli Defense Forces (IDF), 8–9; Arab concerns, 75; defense in depth, 29; grand strategy, 13–15, 17–18

Jericho-IIB missile, 39, 68
Joint Arab Defense Agreement, 47–48
Jordan. *See* Hashemite Kingdom of Jordan
Jordan River, 46

Kamal, Hussein, 25
Khomeini, Ayatollah, 24
Kilo submarines, 59
Kissinger, Henry, 15
Kurds, 15
Kuwait, 44

League of Nations, 37
Lebanese Shiites, 13
Lebanon: Israeli invasion, 13; Israeli-Syrian red lines, 15; peace with Israel and Syria, 3, 55, 85; terrorism, 16; war in, 51
Lebanonization, 12
Libya, 45
low-intensity conflict, 112

Madrid peace process, 20
Maghreb states, 44–46
maritime security-building measures, 81; Iran naval buildup, 59–60
Maronite Christians, 15
mechanized division, 112
MECSF. *See* Middle East Cooperative Security Framework
media, Arab, 23
Meir, Golda, 18
"Memorandum of Understanding Between the Government of the United States and the Government of Israel on Strategic Cooperation," 40
Mershon Center (Ohio State University), 88
Middle East: nuclear weapon–free zone, 61, 112–13; regional definition, 2; regional environment, 19–25, 53–61; U.S. engagement, 93–94, 96; U.S. stabilizing effects, 93–94. *See also specific states*
Middle East Cooperative Security Framework (MECSF), 71, 89–93, 95
Middle East security. *See* security
MiG-21 and MiG-23 aircraft, 51

military capability, 113
military deception, 111–12
military doctrine, 49, 56–57
military objectives, 113
military posture, 113
military strategy: national, 113
minorities: Israeli alliances, 15. *See also specific minority groups*
missiles: Chinese missile boats, 59; war of the cities, 43. *See also* ballistic missiles
Morocco, 45
Mubarak, Hosni, 22
Multilateral Negotiations on the Middle East: remarks by Baker before Organizational Meeting for, 97–101
Multilateral Working Group on Arms Control and Regional Security. *See* Arms Control and Regional Security talks

NAM countries (Non-Alignment Movement countries), 51
Nasser, Gamal Abdel, 9, 16
Nasserism, 23
nationalism, Arab, 23
national military strategy, 113
national security, 113; Arab, 33–72; interests, 113; Israeli, 7–31
national technical means, 27, 113
Netanyahu, Benjamin, 3
Netherlands, 80–81
No-Dong missile, 25
no-first-use declarations, 66
Non-Aligned Movement (NAM) countries, 51
Non-Proliferation Treaty (NPT), 6, 114; Arab concerns, 40, 45, 65, 75; Israeli concerns, 17, 27
North Korea, 25
NPT. *See* Non-Proliferation Treaty
nuclear arms control, 82–84
nuclear weapons, 39–40; Comprehensive Test Ban Treaty, 65–66; Israeli, 11, 16–17, 39, 77; last resort decla-

rations, 66; last resort doctrine, 68,
74–75; no-first-use declarations, 66;
Non-Proliferation Treaty (NPT), 6,
17, 27, 40, 45, 65, 75, 114. *See also*
specific programs
nuclear weapon–free zone, 27, 65;
Middle East, 61, 112–13
NWFZ. *See* nuclear weapon–free zone

Ofeq satellite system, 41
Ohio State University Mershon Center,
88
oil embargo, 50
open-skies arrangements, 29
Open Skies Treaty, 114
operational arms control, 4, 63, 114
operational level of war, 114
order of battle, 114; Israeli, 17
Organizational Meeting for Multilateral
Negotiations on the Middle East: remarks by Baker, 97–101
Osiraq reactor, 18
Oslo agreements, 3, 53–54
Outer Space Treaty, 114

Pact of the League of Arab States, 47
Palestine, 2; Jordan as (myth), 91;
League of Nations' mandate for, 37;
Lebanonization of, 12
Palestine Liberation Organization
(PLO), 45; Declaration of Principles, 3, 86
Palestinian Authority, 3, 55
Palestinian National Council, 53–54
Palestinians: mandate for peace, 54;
right of return, 12
peace: armed, 57, 66; background for,
1–6; between Israel, Syria, and Lebanon, 85; mandate for, 54; milestones, 1–4; preemptive, 21
peace process, 19–21, 53; Arab concerns, 75; bilateral negotiations,
54–56; Camp David Accords,
50–51; Israel-Jordan peace treaty,
63; Madrid, 20; Oslo agreements,

53–54; regional implications, 61;
threats to, 21–25
People's Democratic Republic of
Yemen: Saudi border clashes, 61;
Soviet-Yemeni agreement, 41
Peres, Shimon, 16, 24
Persian Gulf states. *See* Gulf states
PLO. *See* Palestine Liberation Organi-
zation
Ploughshares Fund, 88
policy of diversification of arms sup-
plies, 47–48
preemptive peace, 21
preemptive strikes, 18
prepositioning, 14, 114
PUGWASH, 88

Qatar: Regional Security Center, 5, 81;
Saudi border clashes, 60–61
Quakers, 88

Rabin, Yitzhak, 3, 15, 67
Rarotonga Treaty, 65, 115
Reagan, Ronald, 48
reassurance, 69–71
Red Sea, 42
REDWG (Regional Economic Devel-
opment Working Group), 4
refugees, 100; right of return, 12
Regional Economic Development
Working Group (REDWG), 4
Regional Security Center (RSC), 5, 81,
95; future operations, 86–87
right of return, 12
Rockefeller Foundation, 88
RSC. *See* Regional Security Center
Rushdie, Salman, 24
Russia, 20, 80; Jewish emigration to Is-
rael, 19. *See also* Soviet Union

safeguards: full-scope, 112; IAEA, 27,
112
SAR (search and rescue), 81
The Satanic Verses (Rushdie), 24
satellites: Ofeq system, 41

Saudi Arabia: arms supplies, 48; border clashes, 60–61; oil embargo, 50; U.S. alliance, 52
SDI (Strategic Defense Initiative), 15
search-and-rescue operations, 81
Search for Common Ground, 88
security: Arab concerns, 68–69, 74–76; Arab perceptions of, 34–46; Arab policy, 66–71; assurances, 114–15; collective, 70–71; cooperative, 66, 71; fundamental principles governing relations, 104–5; Israeli concerns, 16, 18, 76–78; Israeli perception of, 7–12; Israeli policy, 28–31; Middle East Cooperative Security Framework, 71, 89–93, 95; national, 113; negative, 66; perceptions of, 78–79, 95; regional environment, 53–61; resolving, 73–96
Shamir, Yitzhak, 34
Shiites, 13
South Pacific Nuclear Free Zone Treaty (Treaty of Rarotonga), 65, 115
Soviet Union: "Agreements of Friendship and Cooperation," 41; Arab states and, 41–42; arms sales to Syria, 54–55; breakup of, 20; economic boycott of Israel, 51–52
START. *See* Strategic Arms Reduction Treaty
Statement on Arms Control and Regional Security, 5–6, 64, 81, 86; text, 103–7
statements of intent, 5
steering committee, 4
strategic advantage, 115
Strategic Arms Reduction Treaty (START), 27, 82; START I Treaty, 115; START II Treaty, 115
strategic cooperation, 40–41
Strategic Defense Initiative (SDI), 15
strategic depth, 84; Arab, 37, 56, 71; Israeli, 9, 17; Arab view of Israeli s.d., 38, 49

strategic deterrence. *See* deterrence
strategic level of war, 115
strategic parity, 48, 51
strategic vulnerability, 37–38, 115
strategy, national military, 113
Sudan, 15, 21
Suez war, 14, 18, 35
surface-to-surface missiles: Iran-Iraq war, 43. *See also* Ballistic missiles
Syria: armed forces, 54–55; arms supplies, 47–48; chemical and biological arms, 25; Damascus Declaration, 60, 70; Gulf War, 54; Israeli-Syrian red lines, 15–16; Israeli-Syrian talks, 3; Madrid peace process, 20; peace with Lebanon and Israel, 54–56, 85; security objectives, 49; Soviet agreement, 41; strategic deterrence, 51; strategic parity, 51; strategic vulnerability, 37–38; terrorism, 16; 1967 war, 10, 13, 36; 1973 war, 10, 14, 49; war in Lebanon, 51

tactical depth, 9, 17, 18, 29, 115
tactical level of war, 115
technical means, national, 113
terrorism, 16, 21–22
Tlatelolco Treaty, 27, 65, 116
track-I talks, 83–84, 116
track-II talks, 84, 116; expansion, 87–89, 95
transparency, 5, 56, 62, 77, 79, 106, 116
Treaty of Rarotonga (South Pacific Nuclear Free Zone Treaty), 65, 115
Treaty of Tlatelolco, 27, 65, 116
Treaty on Conventional Armed Forces in Europe, 82, 116
Tunisia, 45; Regional Security Center, 5, 81
Turkey, 15, 80

UNDOF (United Nations Disengagement Observer Force), 50

UNEF. *See* United Nations Emergency Force
United Arab Emirates, 2
United Kingdom, 36–37; arms control, 61; defense agreements, 60, Suez war, 14, 18, 35
United Nations Charter: Article VII, 93; Article VIII, 90
United Nations Disengagement Observer Force (UNDOF), 50
United Nations Emergency Force (UNEF), 35–36
United Nations General Assembly, 8; Conference on Disarmament, 27–28; Middle East nuclear weapon–free zone proposal, 113; Resolution 181 (II), 37
United Nations Security Council (UNSC): cease-fire resolutions, 35; Resolution 242, 3, 36–37; Resolution 338, 3, 37; Resolution 425, 3; Resolution 426, 3; Resolution 687, 44; Resolution 986, 59
United Nations Special Commission (UNSCOM), 23–25
United States: aid to Egypt, 55; alliance with Saudi Arabia, 52; arms control, 61, 63; arms sales, 48; Ballistic Missile Defense Organization (BMDO), 15, 30, 41; Camp David Accords, 50–51; defense agreements, 60; dual containment policy toward Iran and Iraq, 58–59; Egyptian relations, 50–51; engagement in Middle East, 80, 93–94, 96; Gulf policy, 58–59; Gulf War, 44; Iran–Iraq War, 57–58; oil embargo, 50; plausible deniability, 17; relations with Israel, 14, 20, 35, 40–41, 52; stabilizing effects, 93–94; Strategic Defense Initiative, 15

United States Department of Energy, 88
United States Department of State: Near East Bureau, 2
University of California: Institute on Global Conflict and Cooperation, 88
UNSCOM (United Nations Special Commission), 23–25

verification, 116
vulnerability, strategic, 37–38, 115

war: of attrition, 10, 49; of the cities, 43; operational level, 114; strategic level, 115; tactical level, 115. *See also specific wars*
Warbah island, 44
water, 100
weapons. *See* arms control; *specific weapons*
weapons of last resort, 39; declarations, 66; Israeli doctrine, 68, 74–75
weapons of mass destruction, 11, 25; over-the-horizon threats, 29; verification, 116
weapons-of-mass-destruction–free zone, 27, 65, 78
West Bank, 38
WMD. *See* weapons of mass destruction
WMDFZ (weapons-of-mass-destruction–free zone), 27, 65, 78
working groups, 3–4. *See also specific groups*

Yemen. *See* People's Democratic Republic of Yemen

Zionism, 7–8, 46, 53

About the Authors

SHAI FELDMAN is a senior research fellow at the Center for Science and International Affairs (CSIA) at Harvard University's John F. Kennedy School of Government. For the previous decade and a half, he was a senior research associate at Tel Aviv University's Jaffee Center for Strategic Studies where, beginning in 1989, he directed the Project on Regional Security and Arms Control in the Middle East. Educated at Hebrew University in Jerusalem and awarded the Ph.D. by the University of California at Berkeley, Dr. Feldman is the author of a number of publications. These include *Israeli Nuclear Deterrence: A Strategy for the 1980s* (New York: Columbia University Press, 1982); *Nuclear Weapons and Arms Control in the Middle East* (Cambridge: MIT Press, 1997); and *The Future of U.S.-Israel Strategic Cooperation* (Washington, D.C.: The Washington Institute for Near East Policy, 1996). He coedited, with Ariel Levite, *Arms Control and the New Middle East Security Environment*, Study No. 23, Tel Aviv University, Jaffee Center for Strategic Studies, 1994; and edited *Confidence Building and Verification: Prospects in the Middle East*, Study No. 24, Tel Aviv University, Jaffee Center for Strategic Studies, 1994.

ABDULLAH TOUKAN is science advisor to His Majesty King Hussein of Jordan. He has been the head of the Jordanian Middle East Peace Negotiations Delegation to the Multilateral Arms Control and Regional Security Working Group, and a member of the Jordanian Bilateral Middle East Peace Negotiations Delegation in the Jordanian-Israeli Peace Negotiations dealing with Borders, Territorial Matters, and Security. Dr. Toukan has written a number of articles on issues related to arms control and regional security in the Middle East region. He received his Ph.D. in theoretical nuclear physics from the Massachusetts Institute of Technology.